Mary Ann Bell, EdD
Mary Ann Berry, PhD
James L. Van Roekel, MLS
with Frank Hoffmann

Internet
and
Personal Computing Fads

Pre-publication
REVIEWS,
COMMENTARIES,
EVALUATIONS . . .

"*Internet and Personal Computing Fads* is a straightforward overview of innovations and developments during the Internet era. This book is accessible and well written; ideal for those who wish to gain a basic understanding of the origins and development of the Internet and computer trends."

Mary Carpenter
Librarian,
Council Bluffs Public Library,
Council Bluffs, Iowa

"An encyclopedic look at Internet buzzwords. This book is sure to enlighten even the most savvy. With new terms appearing daily, keeping up with the latest terminology is difficult at best. These pithy entries provide one-stop shopping for the hottest terms. The brief bibliographies also provide more complete information, if needed.

A feature of this book is that not only are there definitions, but coping strategies are also included. How to deal with all these culture benders may be the most outstanding facet of this book."

Carol Simpson, EdD
Assistant Professor,
University of North Texas
School of Library and Information
Sciences

The Haworth Press®
New York • London • Oxford

Internet
and
Personal Computing Fads

THE HAWORTH PRESS
Titles of Related Interest

Internet
and
Personal Computing Fads

Mary Ann Bell, EdD
Mary Ann Berry, PhD
James L. Van Roekel, MLS

with Frank Hoffmann
and assistance from Ryan Crissy

The Haworth Press®
New York • London • Oxford

PUBLISHER'S NOTE
Due to the ever-changing nature of the Internet, Web site names and addresses, though verified to the best of the publisher's ability, should not be accepted as accurate without independent verification.

The Haworth Press, Inc., 10 Alice Street, Binghamton, NY 13904-1580.

Cover design by Jennifer M. Gaska.

Library of Congress Cataloging-in-Publication Data

Bell, Mary Ann, 1946-
    Internet and personal computing fads / Mary Ann Bell, Mary Ann Berry, James Van Roekel; with Frank Hoffmann and assistance from Ryan Crissy.
        p. cm.
    Includes bibliographical references and index.
    ISBN 0-7890-1771-7 (cloth : alk. paper) — ISBN 0-7890-1772-5 (pbk. : alk. paper)
    1. Information society. 2. Internet—Social aspects. 3. Microcomputers. 4. Fads. I. Berry, Mary Ann. II. Van Roekel, James L. III. Title.

HM851.B454 2004
303.48'33—dc21
                                                                        2003009793

CONTENTS

ABOUT THE AUTHORS

Mary Ann Bell, EdD, MLS, is Assistant Professor in the Department of Library Science at Sam Houston State University in Texas, where she teaches classes related to technology and librarianship. She has published and presented at conferences on the topics of information ethics and creative teaching that incorporates technology. Dr. Bell is active in the Texas Library Association, American Library Association, Texas Computer Education Association, Texas Association for Educational Teaching, Association for the Advancement of Computing in Education, and Delta Kappa Gamma. She enjoys nature photography, hiking, and reading.

Mary Ann Berry, PhD, MLS, MSE, is Assistant Professor and Chair of the Department of Library Science at Sam Houston State University in Texas. She has published and presented at numerous conferences. Dr. Berry has served as Chair of the Texas Association for School Librarians, a division of the Texas Library Association, an organization in which she is very active. She is also a member of the American Library Association, Phi Delta Kappa, and numerous local organizations.

James L. Van Roekel, MLS, MA, is Director of Academic Instructional Technology and Distance Learning at Sam Houston State University in Texas. His research, publications, and teaching focus on the investigation of the utilization of free and off-the-shelf hardware and software toward the development of multimedia and digital library applications in distance learning and Web-based broadcasting. He has been awarded two technology grants totaling more than $650,000 toward educating university faculty in thinking about and using technology and technology applications as well as creating multimedia course content. In addition, he has written and presented on these subjects to foster international exchanges with former Communist countries in Eastern Europe. He is a part-time musician, audio engineer and sound designer, photographer, and videographer.

Acknowledgments

We have enjoyed the process of collaboration involved in writing this book, and would like to thank those individuals who were instrumental in helping with the process. First, thanks to Frank Hoffmann, who served as our editor, encourager, advisor, and index specialist. Without him this project would never have been completed. Thanks also to Martin Manning of the U.S. State Department for his invaluable help and guidance in locating illustrations. Librarians at the Library of Congress Prints and Photographs Division were wonderfully welcoming and helpful. Finally, profuse thanks to Ryan Crissy, whose edits, additions, and suggestions were always informed and helpful.

By way of individual thanks, I extend my appreciation to my friends: Debbie Henson for her practical advice, and Barb McGrath for her encouragement. Special thanks to Cindy Traylor for her interest and enthusiasm. Finally, I would like to remember my family, especially my father, Zeb Fitzgerald, who taught me the value of a job well done; my daughter, Emily, who is my muse; and my best friend, Ron Bell, who offered unflagging support.—Mary Ann Bell

Thanks to Frank Hoffmann for asking me to write this book. I am grateful to Cindy Traylor, my secretary, for her help in typing when my computer crashed, and to the faculty of the Library Science Department at Sam Houston State University for their support and encouragement. Thanks to Dr. Herman Totten, my mentor and advisor throughout my doctoral program. Last but not least, thanks to my special daughter, Charee, and my wonderful husband, Bobby, who has been there for me in all my endeavors.—Mary Ann Berry

My heart to Amber and Maddy for all of their patience, support, and love. My thanks to Bob, Pat, Regis, Bonnie, Sarah, Neil, Robby, Ande, Ana, Dan, Lesli, Kevin, Wade, Adam, Ryan, Josh, Matt, Merryn, Ashton, Stacey CR, Stacey RC, Mary, Ed, Frank, Tom, Herbert, Roger, Conk, Roland, Brian, David, Grettle, and Carlton: sometimes my critics, always my teachers and friends.—James Van Roekel

Introduction

This volume is organized in much the same arrangement as others in the multi-volume Haworth fad encyclopedia series, which includes such titles as *Arts and Entertainment Fads, Fashion and Merchandising Fads,* and *Sports and Recreation Fads.* The purpose is to offer a well-documented overview of events and developments relating to the explosion of computer technology and the Internet in American society. As with other books in this series, *Internet and Personal Computing Fads* includes historical and present-day references, and also offers predictions about future trends and fads. The result is a book that provides interesting browsing as well as references in specific terms. Entries are couched in layman's terms, making the book particularly approachable and useful for the "newbie" or novice user of computers and the Internet. This book could be useful in high school and academic libraries, public libraries, and for general use by readers wanting to become more familiar with fads, trends, and events relating to computers and the Internet and the language used to describe them.

Without a doubt, developments in technology have transformed almost all aspects of modern life since the early days of computers, beginning with ENIAC in the 1930s. Computers are ubiquitous in their presence and exert tremendous influence on business, entertainment, and education—just about every aspect of modern life. As computer technology developed, a culture and language grew up around it. Perhaps nothing can prove more dramatically the impact of computers on society than the hysteria surrounding the Y2K problem. Faced with the prospect of massive computer failures, people came to realize just how much they depended on computer technology to make society work. The fact that the problem turned out to be largely a nonevent did not erase the knowledge that computers have tremendous importance in countless arenas.

Further dramatic changes have been wrought by the advent of the World Wide Web. From its humble beginnings in the 1960s as the Department of Defense's Advanced Research Projects Agency Network (ARPANET), the Internet has branched out across the world, growing into a vast network of sites offering every imaginable type of information, from the sublime to the ridiculous. As personal computers decreased in price and increased in memory storage capacity, it became possible for anyone to publish to the Internet, regardless of the quality, authority, or intent of material offered. The result is the chaotic, fascinating, frustrating, and daunting morass of information known today as the World Wide Web. As with the development of computer technology, the growth of the Internet spawned a legion of fads and trends. Terminology to describe new developments can be daunting to anyone attempting to learn how to navigate through cyberspace with any amount of success.

This book offers a layman's guide to the unfamiliar and changing language and latter-day myths that have emerged along with the explosions in computer and Internet use. Criteria for choosing entries for this volume included historical importance, present popularity, and the likelihood that they will play an important part in the future development of computers and the Internet. Well-known and familiar usages are stressed, as opposed to the esoteric. Terms included were selected to represent a variety of fields of interest including general use, business, entertainment, multimedia development, and education. The book offers an interesting retrospective view of the development of computer and Internet use, a description of current fads and trends, and predictions on how the technologies will develop in the future.

Acceptable Use Policy

Many schools and businesses routinely provide and often require computer network access for students and employees. It is generally understood that participants will use the access for intended educational or work-related purposes. However, human nature being what it is, misuse of time and equipment has become a growing concern. To address this problem, many networks have turned to the drafting of an Acceptable Use Policy (AUP).

An AUP is a set of rules and/or procedures that a user must agree to follow in order to be granted network access. Home users generally sign such a policy in order to sign up with an Internet service provider (ISP). Typically, the user agrees to adhere to guidelines such as the following:

- Not using the service to violate any law
- Not attempting to break the security of any computer network or user
- Not posting commercial messages to Usenet groups without prior permission
- Not attempting to send junk e-mail or spam to anyone who does not want to receive it
- Not attempting to mail bomb a site with mass amounts of e-mail in order to flood its server.

AUPs for schools may be instituted for users from the earliest grades through university level. Typically a school policy stresses ethical and educational use of computers and the Internet. Student safety is a priority, as is responsible and constructive use. Consequences for violation of policy may be spelled out as well. The consensus is that schools that offer computer access without having an AUP in place risk practical and possibly illegal problems. As a result, it is increasingly rare to find a school that lacks a policy.

Acceptable use policies are also common in the business world. Employers put them in place to discourage loss of productivity resulting from personal Internet use, to guard against e-mail abuses such as spamming or sending objectionable messages, and to cut down on wasted technical assistance that results from unrestricted access and use. The typical business AUP includes guidelines for employees regarding personal use of e-mail and the Internet, and restrictions on visiting pornographic or hate sites. Although some companies have fired or disciplined employees who violated AUPs, many favor guidelines that are not excessively restrictive and allow some leeway for personal use within defined reasonable parameters. Employees are cautioned that the First Amendment does not apply to use of equipment owned by the business where they work. Because companies own the computers and software, and because employees access them on paid time, employers routinely exercise their rights to restrict and monitor how their computers are used. The use of AUPs offers schools and businesses the means to clarify their policies regarding computer use and also serves as a protection against problems occurring in the event of misuse. As dependence on computer technology increases in schools and the business world, AUPs will play ongoing and growing roles in dictating how the technology should be used.

BIBLIOGRAPHY

Feldman, J. (2001). "It's Not About the Technology." *Network Computing* 12 (June 25), p. 37.

Verton, D. (2000). "Employers OK with Surfing." *Computerworld* 34 (December 18), pp. 1-2.

Wagner, M. (1996). "Firms Spell Out Appropriate Use of Internet for Employees." *Computerworld* (February 5), p. 55.

Artificial Intelligence

"Let's make a machine that can do the work of a person." Not a new idea. A windmill can mill grain and pump water from a cistern. The cotton gin can remove seeds from cotton. A robotic arm can paint automobiles with little human interaction. These machines can operate all day, do not get tired, do not complain, and are easily replaceable. Machines were a boon for the industrial revolution. Machines were a boon for the information revolution. Machines make work easier and more productive as they become smarter. Really? Where are we now?

The MIT Artificial Intelligence (AI) Lab has been in existence since 1959. According to Rodney A. Brooks (2002), director of the lab,

> Our intellectual goal is to understand how the human mind works. We believe that vision, robotics, and language are the keys to understanding intelligence, and as such our laboratory is much more heavily biased in these directions than many other Artificial Intelligence laboratories. Our mode of operation is to attack theoretical issues and application areas at the same time. Even for theory however, we like to build experimental systems to test out ideas.

Brooks describes the thirteen sections of the AI Lab as follows:

- Bio machines
- Computer architecture
- Genomics
- Humanoid robotics
- Information access
- Intelligent working spaces
- Machine learning
- Medical vision
- Mobile robotics

- Reliable software
- Speech
- Vision
- Vision applied to people

When we think of AI, we typically conjure visions of humanoid robots, or androids if you like. This also may include Internet search engines such as Google <http:www.google.com>. Google's Page-Rank program interprets a link from page A to page B as a vote, by page A, for page B; while also analyzing the page that casts the vote. High-quality, high-vote sites receive a higher rank, which Google remembers each time it conducts a search. Google then combines the rank with sophisticated text-matching techniques to locate pages that are both important and relevant to the search.

"The Mind Machine" display was part of a large exhibit at the U.S. Pavilion at the Japanese Tsukuba Expo in 1985, depicting the future of artificial intelligence. Subsequent developments have surpassed the expectations of that time. (*Source: Final Report United States Pavilion Tsukuba Expo '85.* Washington, DC: United States Information Agency, 1985.)

One early example of AI is ELIZA (accessible at <http://www.ai.ijs.si/eliza/eliza.html>), a computerized psychotherapist that gives responses based on human input (i.e., typing). Julia (at <http://www.lazytd.com/lti/julia/>) is another example of a computer program that a human can interact with using an early form of chat. Each of these programs was put to the Turing test. Developed by Alan Turing, the Turing test is a simple experiment in which a machine is declared intelligent based on its ability to converse with a human participant via textual messages and fool the participant into thinking that the machine is human as well.

We may also recall that in 1997, IBM's Deep Blue beat world champion Garry Kasparov at a game of chess. It turns out that the much-publicized bout had more to do with processing power and stamina than skill, in that Deep Blue did not tire and was able to calculate moves much faster than Kasparov. However, Deep Blue does not have an understanding of the game, only formulas to process.

BIBLIOGRAPHY

Brooks, R.A. (2001). *AI Lab Abstracts—2002*. Available at <http://www.ai.mit.edu/research/abstracts/abstracts2002/index.shtml>, accessed September 22, 2003.

Crockett, L. (1994). *The Turing Test and the Frame Problem: AI's Mistaken Understanding of Intelligence*. Norwood, NJ: Intellect Books.

Google (n.d.). *Google Technologies*. Available at <http://www.google.com/technology/index.html>, accessed June 13, 2002.

Bandwidth

When speaking of computers and the Internet, we often hear complaints about bandwidth. There never seems to be enough of it, but just what is it? *Bandwidth* is the amount of data that can move or be transmitted down a given channel. Think of it as a multilane freeway. The more lanes a freeway has, the more traffic it can handle at a faster pace. This is important, especially during rush hours. As lanes are taken away, traffic begins to slow as cars and trucks begin to move into the remaining lanes. As congestion worsens, traffic slows even further. In many instances, an eight-lane freeway suddenly becomes a two-lane freeway, creating a bottleneck. This holds true in bandwidth for computers and the Internet as well. As more users log on, more and more data packets are sent along the same paths. Traffic is especially slowed as big, multitrailer semitrucks carry multimedia-streaming content over the lanes. Bandwidth is not only an issue of traffic, but of the physical "road" as well. Copper lines that were designed to carry voice signals are now required to carry data as well. These lines are noisy and require software-based error control; this, too, slows traffic. A better road is fiber optics. Fiber-optic cables can deliver close to 1,000 billion bits per second, whereas the best copper can achieve is 56,000 bits per second. A fiber about the size of a human hair could transmit a million channels of television simultaneously. Of course, individuals do not yet have access to fiber in their homes. This is why compression is so important. As individual users become increasingly interested in content that is larger and, consequently, slower to download or view, bandwidth must be made to keep up. DSL (digital subscriber lines) and Internet cable services offer about 1.5 million bits per second, though bandwidth drops as more neighborhood users go online.

Bandwidth will continue to increase, but not just over lines—satellite and wireless technologies, too, will see an increase in bandwidth as demand continues to grow. Nicholas Negroponte (1995), founder of MIT's Media Lab, believes that, when dealing with limited bandwidth, it may be better to download an entire program rather than watch it in real time. The content broadcast, therefore, becomes more important than how fast the signal is received.

BIBLIOGRAPHY

Negroponte, N. (1995). *Being Digital*. New York: Vintage Books.

Biometrics

The September 11, 2001, attacks on New York's World Trade Center brought focus on the need to identify potential terrorists or other threatening individuals before they have a chance to strike. The surveillance camera shots of Mohamed Atta and other hijackers as they passed through airport security gave rise to calls for the use of facial scanning to help reduce the chances of known terrorists gaining access to airplanes and other public venues. Biometrics, the science of measuring biological data, is being touted as a powerful tool in crime prevention. Biometrics includes the measurement of fingerprints, facial features, voice patterns, and characteristics of the iris of the eye. Interest in biometrics was high before the World Trade Center attacks, but those events resulted in far greater demand. Currently, the technology for face recognition is effective enough to survey public places and compare faces to existing databases, such as terrorist watch lists. Facial recognition technology could be used in airports, at public buildings and attractions, and at large gatherings such as sporting events or political meetings. According to Brad Grimes (2003), facial recognition cameras were used at the 2001 Super Bowl, comparing faces of fans with a database of mug shots. Grimes also pointed to the increased use of fingerprint recognition by businesses, including American Express at their New York headquarters. As a result, he mused, passwords and ID cards may become passé as biometrics becomes the preferred means of identifying people and granting access to events, buildings, and computer terminals.

In addition to facial scanning, fingerprinting and iris scanning are popular methods of identifying people. These techniques involve knowledge on the part of individuals being checked, who must knowingly offer a print or submit to a scan. By contrast, facial scanning can be conducted without the knowledge or permission of people in a crowd. For a number of years, parents have participated in drives to fingerprint their children as a precaution in case a child is lost or abducted and needs to be identified quickly and easily. Thumbprints are used by banks and credit agencies for customer identification. Iris scanning is a growing means of identifying people to be admitted into secure buildings or rooms at government or corporate sites.

The use of biometrics is not without complications. Facial scanning can be inaccurate and result in cases of mistaken identity. Further, in order for a potential offender to be caught, he or she must be recognized as such. If a terrorist has managed to stay off watch lists, facial scanning is useless without the necessary reference. Having the equipment in place might create a false sense of security and cause personnel to depend less on other means of checking for threatening individuals.

In addition, the specter of invasion of privacy exists. Facial scanning, done in secret, could easily be used to keep track of people for reasons other than security. In the wrong hands, predators could even use it to stalk innocent victims. Biometric data gathering will doubtless be important in the arsenal of tools used in the war against terrorism. It should be one of many tools, and people need to be aware of potential abuses as well as uses.

BIBLIOGRAPHY

Grimes, B. (2003). "Biometric Security." *PC Magazine* 22 (April 22), p. 74.

Stikeman, A. (2001). "Recognizing the Enemy." *Technology Review* 104 (December), pp. 48-50.

Violino, B. (1997). "Trends: Biometrics—Body Language—Fingerprints, Faces, Even Eyes Are the New Keys to Protecting Secure Systems." *Information Week* (August 18), p. 36.

Blogging

Blogging is an increasingly popular mode of self-expression that started via the Internet in the late 1990s. The term *blogging* is an abbreviation for "Web logging," and refers to the practice of posting brief entries to the Internet about topics of interest or concern to the author. Postings range from personal diaristic entries to pronouncements about controversial issues or reports of news events. Styles range from casual and personal to more formal and journalistic.

To illustrate the rapid growth of this trend, blogging historian Rebecca Blood reported that only twenty-three Web logs existed in 1999, whereas between 500,000 and 1 million existed by 2002 (Conhaim, 2002). Some bloggers seek to keep online journals of their personal lives. They may describe mundane activities such as shopping excursions, vacations, or evenings out, or may unburden themselves with accounts of trials and tribulations that rival the events of any soap opera. Entertainers, especially those trying to launch careers, may make blogging part of their Web sites in hopes of connecting with fans.

Most bloggers use specialized software available on the Internet at no charge or for minimal fees. A simple Web search can identify numerous sites that allow users to set up new accounts. Once an account is created, it is just a matter of a few clicks to set up a personal page. The ease of getting online in this manner is part of the appeal.

Writers who have a journalistic or iconoclastic bent have taken the practice of blogging to another level. Their purposes tend to be to write political commentary, to promote a favorite cause, or to report news events. Since bloggers do not operate under the same constraints regarding verification of sources, they can publish extremely quickly and have scored some journalistic coups by getting stories out well before they appear in traditional media sources. As bloggers gain readership and recognition, it is likely that prominent bloggers will have a greater impact in the world of journalism. A prime example of this influence is Harry Knowles' Web site, *Ain't It Cool News* (http://www.aintitcool.com/), which offers news, opinions, and gossip about new and upcoming movies and entertainment personalities. According to Gillian Flynn (2002), Knowles is so feared by producers that he gets invitations, complete with private jet trips, to early movie screenings. In fact, his prerelease criticism of the movie *Rollerball* (2002) delayed production and sent the film into reshoots. Whether personal or public, the practice of blogging is a form of e-publishing that is growing in popularity and influence.

BIBLIOGRAPHY

Conhaim, W. (2002). "Blogging—What Is It?" *Link-Up* 3 (May 1), pp. 3-6.
Flynn, G. (2002). "Prince Harry." *Entertainment Weekly* 640 (February 22), pp. 8-9.
Leo, J. (2002). "A Blog's Bark Has Bite." *U.S. News and World Report* (May 13), p. 48.
Taylor, C. (2002). "Psst. Wanna See My Blog? Impromptu Online Journals Are Popping Up All Over the Web." *Time* 159 (February 11), p. 68.

Bookmarks

Once a hard-to-find Internet site is located, the last thing a diligent searcher wants to do is lose it again. The easiest and quickest way to keep up with preferred sites is to use bookmarks. A *bookmark* is a saved link to an Internet site that has been added to a compilation of other marked sites. Different Internet browsers may employ different titles—Internet Explorer uses the term *favorite,* whereas Netscape and other browsers use the term *bookmark.*

Bookmarks can be helpful when they are used sparingly, or problematic when the list gets too long. It is easy to accumulate hundreds, or even thousands of bookmarks, thus virtually negating their usefulness. Browser software can help with bookmark organization by allowing the user to create folders, assign subject headings, and alphabetize bookmarks.

Specialized applications on the market further facilitate bookmark management. Such applications promise to find duplicates, organize by key word, and test for current validity. Anyone with a very long list of bookmarks might want to explore such tools. There are also free Internet sites that allow subscribers to post bookmarks, thereby making them available from any computer. Such a site can also serve as a backup to protect against loss or corruption of bookmarks, and help the user who switches between browsers or between computers.

Whether one's needs call for a separate management program or online storage depends on an individual's needs. As in many things, moderation is probably the key to enjoying maximum use from bookmarks. Used judiciously and sparingly, they are excellent aides in Internet searching.

BIBLIOGRAPHY

Lanza, S. (2001). "Bookmarks: Our Unruly, Unmanageable Friends." *Searcher* 9 (March), pp. 48-53.

Whatis.com (2002). "Bookmark." In *Whatis?com's Encyclopedia of Technology Terms.* Indianapolis, IN: Que.

Bots

Sometimes called "agents," *bots* are small programs that run across a network and execute information gathering or processing tasks on behalf of the user. These are repetitive tasks that are typically run several times on a schedule and are very often used in e-commerce, Web-site administration, and software distribution. Web spiders are bots that search Web sites, read information, and create entries for Web search engines. Think of Web spiders as indexers. Bots such as ELIZA and Julia are examples of artificial intelligence (see ARTIFICIAL INTELLIGENCE).

Bots have existed since the 1960s and are guided by algorithmic rules of behavior, i.e., "if this happens, then do this, or else this"; similar to an electronic flowchart. The term *bot* is obviously derived from the term *robot,* first coined by Czech science fiction author Karel Capek to describe mechanical beings; it is literally translated as "forced labor."

Primarily used by Internet shoppers to find the best price for an item (shop bots), bots also include search engines (search bots), artificial life bots, tracking and surfing bots, e-mail filter bots, and advertising bots. Bots can update your stock portfolio, remind you of calendar events, find restaurants and movies, and share files—anything that can be automated on a computer. Bots are not just used on the Internet. Computer users can run bots locally on their desktops and laptops. Such bots can be configured to perform "menial" tasks, such as searching for and irradiating viruses, defragmenting hard drives, and checking for junk e-mail.

Not all bots are good, however. A more malicious bot can make an instant copy of a Web site's data, including content and account numbers. A bot can also slow down a site by searching it faster than the server can serve pages, finally causing the server to crash. In 2000, online auction site eBay took its competitor Bidder's Edge to court for sending bots to crawl the eBay site. A federal judge granted an injunction against Bidder's Edge, based on eBay's use of the Robot Exclusion Standard. As its name suggests, the Robot Exclusion Standard was created to govern bots without human supervision.

Robots employed by the average technology user are not the giant metallic humanoid machines from 1950s science fiction B-movies; they are software-based entities that still do forced labor.

BIBLIOGRAPHY

Leonard, A. (1997). *Bots: The Origin of New Species*. San Francisco: Hardwired.
Luh, J.C. (2001). "No Bots Allowed." *Interactive Week* 8(15) (April 16), p. 62.

CAD

In 1957, Dr. Patrick J. Hanratty, known as "the father of CAD," developed PRONTO, the first numerical-control programming system. The first CAD, or computer aided or assisted design, used simple algorithms to display patterns in two dimensions (2-D). In March 1965, Donald Welbourn was given a grant by the Science Research Council with which to start work on CAD, and it was he who saw the possibility of using the computer to assist in modeling 3-D shapes. In 1971, Hanratty founded Manufacturing and Consulting Services, Inc., which developed the first commercially available CAD product. Mike and Tom Lazear are credited with developing the first personal computer CAD software in 1979. From the 1980s to the present, the software has undergone many changes, but the basic concept has stayed the same.

CAD is a combination hardware and software program used by various groups and individuals, including architects, engineers, drafters, and artists, to create precision drawings or technical illustrations. According to Webopedia.com (n.d.), "It gives a design view from any angle with a push of a button and zoom in for close-ups and long-distance views." Variations of the original software program are used in many fields.

The PCASE (Pavement-Transportation Computer Assisted Structural Engineering) project was established recently to develop and provide computer programs for use in the design and evaluation of transportation systems. The application of this program will save time and money in the development of future systems.

Many CAD professional associations exist, including the American Association of Engineering Societies, Association for Computer Aided Design Architecture, American Institute of Architects, American Concrete Institute, American Council for Construction Education, American Institute of Building Design, and the Engineered Wood Association, which gives an idea of the variety of users for this program. Several journals are devoted to this topic, including *The*

CAD Digest: The Reading Room for Computer Aided Design and *CADSystems Online Magazine.*

In April 2002, two Canadian high schools were among the winners of the Autodesk Inventor Award and the Autodesk Visualization Award at the First Robotics Competition Championship event held at Walt Disney World's Epcot Center in Orlando, Florida. Some students used Unigraphics' computer-aided design and manufacturing software to create a computer-simulated design of the world's first rocket car.

In the future this software program will be used in a broader variety of fields.

BIBLIOGRAPHY

Bozdoc, M. (2002). "The History of CAD." *Resources and Information for Professional Designers.* Available from <http://mbinfo.digitalrice.com/>.

CAD Systems. (n.d.). *CADSystems Online Magazine.* Available from <http://www.cadsystems.com>.

PCASE Committee (2002). "PCASE 2.0." Available from <http://www.pcase.com>.

TenLinks, Inc. (2003). "Cad Organizations." Available from <http://www.tenlinks.com/CAD/reference/organizations.htm>.

Webopedia.com (n.d.). "CAD." Available from <http://www.webopedia.com/TERM/C/CAD.html>.

Whatis.com (n.d.). "CAD." Available from <http://searchvb.techtarget.com/sDefinition/0,,sid8_gci211732,00.html>.

Chat and E-Mail Abbreviations

Shorthand was a method devised centuries ago to transcribe material in a speedier manner. This idea has been carried forward today in the abbreviations we use for e-mail, Internet chat, and instant messaging. Most people are familiar with such expressions as TGIF (thank God it's Friday) or FYI (for your information). In order to save time and for speed, communications via the Internet have adopted some of these same abbreviations. Others have been added, and the list today is quite lengthy. They range from businesslike to playful, and are sometimes a bit naughty. With the use of pagers and cellular telephones, abbreviations have become more commonplace and useful. As a result, users employ an ever-growing list of expressions. Common examples include:

BBL	Be back later	LOL	Laughing out loud
BTW	By the way	NP	No problem
CU	See you	PDA	Public display of affection
DQMOT	Don't quote me on this		
EOM	End of message	ROTFL	Rolling on the floor laughing
F2F	Face to face		
FYI	For your information	TIA	Thanks in advance
GAL	Get a life	TMI	Too much information
HTH	Hope this helps	TTFN	Ta-ta for now
IC	I see	TTYL	Talk to you later
IMHO	In my humble opinion	WTG	Way to go
ILY	I love you	WU?	What's up?
IRL	In real life (as opposed to chatting)		

BIBLIOGRAPHY

Park, K. (2001). "Internet Lingo." *World Almanac and Book of Facts, 2001.* New York: World Almanac Books.

Whatis.com (2001). "Chat abbreviations." *Whatis?com's Encyclopedia of Technology Terms.* Indianapolis, IN: Que, pp. 120-122.

Chat Rooms

A *chat room* is an Internet discussion area. "It can be a Web site, part of a Web site, or part of an online service, such as America Online (AOL)" (Deltabrook, n.d.). Soon after William Gibson coined the term *cyperspace,* the growing Internet and new commercial online services created "places" or "rooms" one could enter to interact with other people; places where people of like mindedness, also called communities, could meet and discuss common areas of interest.

Joining a chat room is relatively easy. Users must first register, choose a name and password, and log into the chat room they prefer. Once in the chat room the user can post messages that are viewable by everyone who is logged into that chat room, or the user can simply read all the information without posting. This is known as lurking. Protecting one's privacy is always important. Know with whom you are speaking and keep it professional.

In July 1999 AOL reported 750 million daily instant messages. Compare this with the 500,000 letters the post office handles daily. By 2000 more than 130 million users worldwide were sending roughly one billion messages per day. It is obvious that instant messages will be the wave of the future.

Potential abuse exists for chat rooms. This includes monopolizing conversations, belittling comments made by others, or scrolling. Some abuse may be unintentional, but is still disruptive to other users. A Federal Trade Commission (FTC) report indicates that many children surfing the Web claim to have experienced problems such as attempted password theft and inappropriate advances by adults in children's chat rooms. The report further states that "traditionally, parents have instructed children to avoid corresponding with strangers; yet the collecting or posting of personal information in chat rooms and on bulletin boards runs contrary to that traditional safety message" (FTC, 1988).

"Chat rooms can be found that focus on virtually any aspect of human endeavor or interest, including classic movies, Irish ancestry, baton twirling, and psychic readings" (Deltabrook, n.d.). Many sites will guide a user through the steps required to create his or her own chat room if one does not exist on the topic of interest. Chat rooms are great for tapping into the global mind and have much value.

BIBLIOGRAPHY

About.com (n.d.). "Chat Room." Available from <http://netforbeginners.about.com/library/glossary/bldef-chatroom.htm>.

Cairncross, F. (2001). *The Death of Distance: How the Communications Revolution Is Changing Our Lives.* Boston, MA: Harvard Business School Press.

Deltabrook (n.d.). "Chat Rooms." Available from <http://www.deltabrook.com/chatrooms.htm>.

Federal Trade Commission (1998). *Privacy Online: A Report to Congress.* Available from <http://www.ftc.gov/reports/privacy3/priv-23.htm>.

Lunenfeld, P. (Ed.) (1999). *The Digital Dialectic: New Essays on New Media.* Cambridge, MA: The MIT Press.

Clip Art

Clip art can be a great time-saver for the busy desktop publisher or Internet Webmaster. The term *clip art* refers to artwork that can be freely copied and published. Long the mainstay of newspaper advertising, clip art is in great demand in the visually driven world of Web pages and computer-generated publications.

One consideration regarding clip art is that the user must avoid violating copyright law when reproducing images. Unfortunately, many Internet users labor under the misconception that anything available and capable of being copied from the Internet is free. To the contrary, publishing an Internet page results in its contents being copyrighted de facto, whether or not symbols or legal announcements to that effect are present. The best protection from this is to use commercially available collections of graphics, many of which are available and reasonably priced, and some of which come along with other software. Many free clip art sites on the Internet offer public domain and royalty free art. In order to make sure it is all right to use images from a site, the user should carefully read the guidelines for use and contact the Web master for clarification or permission when in doubt. Using clip art is an excellent way to make computer generated projects and documents interesting and attractive.

BIBLIOGRAPHY

Georgia, B. (1999). "Eliminate Time Wasters." *PC Computing* 12 (September), pp. 230-233.

Comic Sites

Comic creators are discovering new challenges and opportunities as they begin to animate their creations online. Editorial cartoonists who originally published their still works online began in the late 1990s to publish animated creations as well. One cartoonist, Pulitzer Prize-winner Clay Bennett, stated, "I can see why Dr. Frankenstein got so excited when his monster came to life. Creating this animation is a lot of fun" (Astor, 1997, p. 36). Bennett's cartoons are quick to download and rely on two to four panel changes, always with a political statement.

Traditional comic book storytellers are turning to the Internet to distribute their animated stories, which have many similarities to the comic books of old, with characters that appear in continuing episodes. Stan Lee, a writer who first made his mark with his Marvel Comic creations, is enthusiastic about the new way of making comics for the Web. Subjects range from action adventures, to the exploits of pop entertainers such as the Backstreet Boys, to slapstick humor.

Teens and twenty-somethings are apt to be fans of small, independent Internet comic sites, a growing genre of animated Internet sites. These sites, like those of more famous comic creations, tend to build around a set of characters that are players in animated sequences. They are often irreverent and offbeat in their humorous situations and characters. Sites offer episodes featuring the adventures and misadventures of their characters. Games are often offered as well, again using the site's characters. Products such as T-shirts, mugs, mouse pads, etc., with the comic logos and characters may be offered for sale. Fans frequently communicate with one another and with the Webmasters via electronic mailing lists or message boards. These sites are developed with the use of animation software. Some of the most established and long-lasting Web comics include *Shawks,* a series in which plucky kids fight off efforts by evil sharks to take over the world, and *Homestar Runner,* with its cast of wacky characters, such as Homestar Runner, Strong Bad, and Marzipan. *Shawks* has even inspired its fans to clamor for a TV version of the popular series. However, co-creator Ed Anderson announced in summer 2003 that Fox TV rejected it as "too violent."

BIBLIOGRAPHY

Astor, D. (1997). "His Latest Creation Is Web Animation." *Editor and Publisher* 130 (September 6), p. 36.
Bennett, C. (n.d.). *The Editorial Cartoons of Clay Bennett.* Available from <http://claybennett.com>.
Homestar Runner (n.d.). Available from <http://www.homestarrunner.com>.
Poniewozik, J. (2000). "Look Up on the Net! It's . . . Cyber Comics!" *Time* 155 (February 14), pp. 76-78.
Shawks (n.d.). Available from <http://www.shawks.net>.
The Stan Lee Resurrection (n.d.). Available from <http://stanleereturns.sourceforge.net/>.

Commercialization

In a capitalist society, one would expect to see *any* opportunity to make money as a great opportunity. Some, myself included, remember a better time in the age of the Internet. The "Information Superhighway" was just that. Researchers used the Net to collaborate and communicate across institutions. When the "Information Superhighway" was first opened to the masses, we still shared everything. No one worried whether someone else "borrowed" a picture or icon from another's page, or whether someone "copped" your code. Then Citibank, Disney, and McDonald's started cruising. Now the "Superhighway" is strung with banks, fast-food chains, brokerages, and malls of every sort. One informal study showed that in 1995, media outlets were transfixed with the Internet as an amazing source of knowledge. Major newspapers in the United States and abroad referred to the "Information Superhighway" in 4,562 stories, and articles mentioned "e-commerce" or "electronic commerce" only 915 times. One year later, coverage of the Internet as an information superhighway fell to 2,370 stories in major newspapers—about half the previous year's level, while coverage of electronic commerce nearly doubled, with mentions in 1,662 articles. In 1999, the media changed focus from information superhighway imagery, with only 842 mentions in major papers, to mentions of e-commerce in 20,641 articles.

It is certainly handy to pay bills online, purchase movie tickets, read and buy books and articles. Online auction sites, such as eBay, are a huge boon too.

The commercialization of the Internet has led to the development of a new Internet, or Internet II. The Internet II will return to the roots of the original Internet, with sharing and collaboration being the focus. It will link universities, research institutions, and any other entity willing to pay for a subscription.

BIBLIOGRAPHY

Solomon, N. (2000). "What Happened to the 'Information Superhighway'?" *The Humanist* 62(2) (March/April), p. 3.

Compression

As technology improves, file sizes, content streams, and signals become increasingly larger. While storage and bandwidth are allowing for more space and traffic, bandwidth is always an issue. *Bandwidth* refers to the available area for electronic traffic over any system or network. Because bandwidth and space are defined by a finite amount, it is important to keep files and streams as small as possible without losing too much quality. This is where compression comes in as a tool. We use codecs to compress information for broadcast. A codec is a software program that compresses (co) and decompresses (dec) the information. Examples of programs that use codecs are Windows Media Player, QuickTime, RealAudio, and MP3.

First, let us examine a bit of how compression works using the following model of the words "cat," "hat," "fat," and "bat." These words represent files and streams. A codec looks for similarities and repeated information. In this case, the repeated information is "at." Because "at" appears four times in our list, we can save some space by removing three and remembering that each time we see "f," "h," "c," or "b," we should use "at" to complete the word. This is a simple explanation of how compression works. By removing duplicate information and keeping track of what other information should precede the duplicates, a lot of space can be saved. Processes are slowed a bit because it takes time to reconnect the proper information.

Using too many different codecs presents problems, however. Though the ability of codecs to compress audio and video data has revolutionized the use of telecommunications bandwidth, in streaming from the source to the end-user it is not unusual for a signal to go through many different codecs along the way. The cumulative effect of this compression, each designed for only a single cycle of compression and decompression and not for an entire series of cycles, can add noise and errors. Because of the difference in codecs, this noise may be seen as important information by another codec, thus making for an undesirable file or stream. This is not only problematic for those who have paid for a music or video download and are expecting a certain degree of quality, but, in a more important scenario, for those who are communicating via voice or video in a conference in which important decisions are being made. In this respect, if noise is introduced into the signal, then the received message contains distortions, errors, and extraneous material that could affect the message's meaning.

Problems aside, compression offers opportunities to share information with a broader audience. Thanks to compression/decompression software, we can download music albums, send home videos or e-mail, and see each other via live webcams. As Web-based television becomes more standardized, we will have the ability to view content from anywhere using current and emerging broadcast technologies.

BIBLIOGRAPHY

Pohlman, K.C. (2002). "One Too Many Codecs." *Sound and Vision* 67(6) (July/August), p. 37.

Shannon, C.E. and Weaver, W. (1963). *The Mathematical Theory of Communication.* Chicago: University of Illinois Press.

Computer Dating

Computer dating—modern day matchmaker or recipe for disaster? The answer is probably both. The concept of finding that special someone with the assistance of computer technology is not new. As early as 1962, columnist Russell Baker described a phenomenon on New England college campuses, in which students turned to a "compatibility research" group for help finding a companion. Since that time the fad waxed and waned, enjoying particular popularity with collegians.

As computers gained importance for communication, the proliferation of ways to meet people online also increased. Paid or subscription services, some touting security based on screening and hefty fees, are one option for online meeting of members of the opposite sex. Typically, the subscriber applies for membership and, ostensibly, is admitted after identity and security checks are made. The fees are another protection in that they tend to discourage casual users. The new member fills out a profile and may offer pictures or a video interview. Members receive profiles based on their responses as evaluated and matched by a computer. Identities are protected until participants mutually agree to meet.

For the more adventurous, chat rooms, message boards, and countless other venues exist. Internet sites invite people with common interests, ranging from the love of gardening to pornography, to get acquainted. Internet chat can offer specific areas, or rooms, in which people can gather for discourse—raunchy or otherwise. One famous online romance was that of right-wing personality Rush Limbaugh. In 1990 he began e-mail correspondence with Marta Fitzgerald, a student at the University of North Florida who wanted advice about dealing with a liberal history professor. They began dating in 1992 and were married in 1994.

Of course there are downsides to the trend of cyber romance. The anonymity of contacts makes it an easy and irresistible avenue for fraud or worse. Con artists abound on the Internet, and lonely people are likely to become easy prey. Advice columnist Ann Landers repeatedly warned people of the dangers of online affairs. Sadder but wiser seekers have reported horror stories of being financially bilked. Worse yet, sexual predators are well known to be skilled in duping victims of all ages.

Even when the repercussions of an online relationship are not dire, they may be disappointing. The long-awaited face-to-face meeting may cause romance to fizzle when the self-described fitness fanatic turns out to be overweight and balding. The person who is eloquent and witty in chat rooms or e-mail may prove annoying or dull in person.

Another area of concern regarding cyber romance is where and when the communication takes place. Businesses are cracking down on cyber flirtation in the workplace, whether it be visiting sexually oriented Web sites or communicating by chat or e-mail. Management is reminding employees that everything they write on company computers belongs to that company and is not private. Communicating electronically from home, while ostensibly casual and frivolous, can lead to marital disaster if the time devoted to it robs the participant's family of time and attention.

Online communication, whether it be for business, education, keeping up with family and friends, or romance, is here to stay. As with any means of venturing into human relationships, it is fraught with perils as well as promise. People who participate will do well to proceed with equal parts caution and enthusiasm.

BIBLIOGRAPHY

Hamilton, J. (1999). "When Cupid Uses a Cursor." *Business Week* 36 (February 22), p. 26.

Stein, M. "Landers Takes on Online Romances." *Editor and Publisher* 129 (August 10), p. 33.

"Walking the Walk." (1994). *People* 41 (June 13), p. 70.

Computer Simulation

What is real and what is not? With computer simulations today the distinction between the two is becoming more and more difficult to discern. What is computer simulation? Its name implies the essence. According to one definition it is "a computer model of a real phenomenon or system in which a 3D simulation is described by 3D models in a computer program" (About.com, n.d.) The diverse use of computer simulation is seen in the wealth of material available on the topic, from games of all sorts, to the field of medicine, to training programs (flight simulators), and information from scientists who "recreate, project into the future and predict real world phenomena" (About.com, n.d.).

Computer simulation can trace its roots to 1968, when Dr. David Evans, founder of the University of Utah's computer science department, and Ivan Sutherland, a computer science professor, founded the Evans & Sutherland Computer Corporation on the campus of the University of Utah. From the beginning, both men believed that computers could be used as simulators. In the 1970s they established a partnership with Rediffusion, a British simulation company that trained commercial airline pilots using flight training simulators. In 1994, Dr. Evans retired, but the company is still playing a role as a pioneer and innovator in its field.

In April 2000, scientists at the Los Alamos and Sandia national laboratories detonated the world's first "e-bomb," a computer-simulated nuclear explosion. By simulating detonations, researchers are able to study the safety and security of nuclear weapons without violating the 1992 nuclear test ban, and are able to do so without harming the environment. However, one problem scientists encountered during their simulation was computing power, or rather the lack of it. Detonating the "e-bomb" required twelve teraflops (one million computations per second), which isn't enough for future needs according to scientists at Los Alamos. A thirty-teraflop supercomputer was scheduled to be installed and running at Los Alamos sometime in 2003 (Hulme, 2002).

Organizations and journals devoted to computer simulations have existed nearly as long as the topic itself. Organizations such as the Society for Computer Simulation International hold annual conferences where one can learn about the latest developments in computer simulation.

BIBLIOGRAPHY

About.com (n.d.). "Simulation." Available from <http://3dgraphics.about.com/library/glossary/bldef-simulation.htm>.

Bleek, P.C. (2000). "DOE Simulates Nuclear Explosion; GAO Faults Ignition Facility." *Arms Control Today* (September). Available from <http://www.armscontrol.org/act/2000_09/doesept00.asp>.

Evans & Sutherland Corp. (n.d.). "History." Available from <http://www.es.com/about_eands/history/index.asp>.

Hulme, G.V. (2002). "Simulations Go Nuclear." *Information Week* (April 8). Available from <http://www.informationweek.com/shared/printableArticle.jhtml?articleID=6502149>.

Computer Visualization

Begin a conversation about computer visualization and most people will think in terms of the HAL 9000 from *2001: A Space Odyssey* (1968). HAL, as the computer was called for short, controlled all aspects of the spaceship's operating functions, from navigation to life support. HAL also conversed with the ship's inhabitants and could respond verbally. The most interesting aspect of HAL was, of course, "his" ability to see; in one instance Hal asked Dave (spaceship operator played by Keir Dullea) to show him the sketch pad Dave was drawing in and commented on the drawings.

In reality, though, *computer visualization* refers to the display of digital information on a computer screen. A simple example is that of radar data readouts on an air traffic controller's display. In this, the controllers see a representation of airplanes, their altitudes, speeds, and directions. A more typical example is that of geographic information systems (GIS), which display modelings of digital maps in manipulating spatial information. Visualization shows relationships that would otherwise be not as evident and, certainly, more difficult to demonstrate as raw data. These relationships show patterns in the chaos; gems in the dross.

Scientists continually use this tool to explore how substances flow around structures. This information can significantly impact the operation of any number of structures. Historians also use computer visualization as a simulation tool for analyzing the growth of historic cities. Such cities can be electronically rebuilt and animated in a way that modern people may experience life as it may have happened in the past. In fact, many university professors use visualization as a lab tool in situations where harmful or toxic materials may not be used in an educational environment. Students can mix chemicals and try physics or engineering projects without the danger, time, or expense that real-world experiments would encounter. In fact, many distance-learning instructors use this as a tool when students do not have access to learning labs. Computer visualizations can also replicate the growth of plants and animals in a short, time-lapse-style frame. These tools can display simulations of practically any sort, using data of varying complexities.

Another example of computer visualization is that of virtual reality. While certainly very popular in the computer gaming industry, virtual reality has grown to be used in flight training, military exercises, and even surgery. As this technology becomes increasingly inexpensive and available, expect to see many uses on the Internet and in the home.

BIBLIOGRAPHY

Achleitner, H.K. and Wyatt, R.B. (1992). "Visualization: A New Conceptual Lens for Research." In J.D. Glazier and R.R. Powell (eds.), *Qualitative Research in Information Management* (pp. 21-36). Englewood, CO: Libraries Unlimited.

Al Sayyad, N. (1999). "Virtual Cairo: An Urban Historian's View of Computer Simulation." *Leonardo* 32(2), pp. 93-101.

Hurwitz, C.L. (1999). "A Teacher's Perspective on Technology in the Classroom: Computer Visualization, Concept Maps and Learning Logs." *Journal of Education* 181(2), pp. 123-128.

Mahoney, D.P. (2001). "Fluid Motion in Focus." *Computer Graphics World* 24(1) (January), pp. 16-18.

Convergence

As technology evolves, more devices offer increased capacity across formats, media, and capabilities. As Roger Wyatt's Technology Quintet model illustrates, video, audio, computers, mass storage, and telecommunications (the five technologies of the quintet) interact toward virtually complete convergence. In this model each member of the quintet can be viewed as a circle whose boundaries are not crisp or static. Their fluidity can be traced as time progresses, where each circle converges to complete or near-complete overlap.

Some practical examples of devices that offer this increased capacity are the latest generation of cell phones. These new phones offer access to telecommunications, MP3 (electronic music) players, e-mail, chat messaging, Internet access, and, in some cases (as with the Nokia 9290 Communicator), video playback. As a device, television has included audio and video, but now allows for Internet access, e-mail, and mass storage in conjunction with hard disk VCRs, such as TIVO. Personal digital assistants (PDAs) and handheld computers are following suit; including MP3 players, built-in digital cameras, video playback, Internet access, and e-mail capabilities. Some of these handheld operating systems are included in cell phone technology. Computers, themselves, are in a continual state of convergence. Millions use computers as Internet devices, mass storage servers for file sharing, music and video creation, production, and broadcast; in fact, many computers have television reception (via cable or satellite). Refrigerators are now being sold that can connect to the Internet for e-mail and recipe databases. Where will this take us?

It's obvious from the preceding examples that convergence in technology is all encompassing. It is also interesting that these devices are beginning to evolve in the same way, offering the same capabilities across devices. As convergence of capabilities becomes standardized, we will begin to see new devices with new capabilities beyond Wyatt's model. This will be exciting to see.

BIBLIOGRAPHY

Wyatt, R.B. (1996). "Digital Cinema Principles and Techniques for Multimedia Development." In R. Griffin (ed.), *VisionQuest: Journeys Toward Visual Literacy: Proceedings of the 1996 IVLA Conference.* College Park, PA: International Visual Literacy Association.

Cookies

Cookies were once what children looked forward to with milk for midmorning or after-school snacks. In the world of the Internet, however, the term *cookie* takes on a whole new meaning. In cyberspace, a *cookie* is a small amount of information that is put on a computer hard drive by and from a Web site. Without cookies in place, each visit to a given Web page is treated as a unique event, with the server having no information about previous visits. Cookies store information about previous visits, enabling pages to load more quickly on subsequent visits and to appear with varying degrees of customization. The information stored is typically something about the user that the instigating server wants to remember for future reference. Once installed, cookies perform such tasks as rotating banner ads at a given site, customizing pages based on the browser being used, etc. Cookies are stored in various locations on a computer's hard drive, depending on the browser used, and can be located by searching the drive.

The concerned user might ask, "What if I do not want these cookies? They are being given without my asking!" The benefits of cookies are that they allow the user to view and utilize Web sites more effectively. The downside can be that some cookies contain profiling information about a user and thus can be viewed as an invasion of privacy. The careful user can opt to delete or throw away cookies from time to time. It is also possible to set one's browser to reject all cookies, but this will cause some Web sites not to load. Throwing away cookies is not a permanent solution, because Web sites will simply add them again when they are visited the next time. To fill the need for managing cookies, companies provide cookie management programs. They do this by methods such as replacing commercially planted cookies with generic code or by helping clean out a user's cache on a regular basis.

It is probably true that in today's Internet world, total anonymity is a myth. Many cookies are innocuous and actually helpful applications. At the same time, it is prudent to be aware of these programs and exercise some control over them.

BIBLIOGRAPHY

Whatis.com (2002). "Cookie." *Whatis?com's Encyclopedia of Technology Terms.* Indianapolis, IN: Que.

Copyright

The purpose of copyright laws is to ensure that the owners of materials are protected from theft and misuse. Twenty years ago copyright law was a subject of interest to a fairly limited number of people whose interests were involved because of their possession and use of print materials. The advent of digital technology has moved the issue into the homes, dorm rooms, and offices of thousands of people. Today the Internet has provided a path for the dissemination of digital copies of sound files, movies, TV shows, images, and other creations in addition to print. It has also made it easy and convenient to copy and share these files for free, a development which Hollywood executives and other distributors say is costing them millions of dollars in lost revenues.

The music industry was the first to cry foul regarding copyright and computers, complaining that Napster, a free Internet sharing service, was dramatically cutting into their revenues. The courts agreed, and lawsuits brought against Napster resulted in measures that hobbled the practices of all services that enabled and encouraged the sharing of music files without payment. The next arena for contention was the distribution of software that allows users to store large banks of movies, TV shows, and collections and then swap them with others. Again industry leaders sounded a hue and cry to bring the same limitations to file sharing of these files as were imposed on Napster and other similar companies.

In addition to taking legal measures, content owners have also sought ways to block the technologies that allow file sharing. One way to do this is by encryption, which results in scrambling files and rendering them useless unless paid for. Another protection that pits content owners against those who would acquire products without paying is digital watermarking. Digital watermarking makes it harder to copy cable and satellite broadcasts as well as Internet images and files.

At the same time that content owners are trying to protect their property through legal and technological measures, consumers are campaigning for their rights to materials. Copying files for later viewing has long been held to be legal, but some measures hamper this capability. Furthermore, buyers argue that owners have brought piracy upon themselves by overcharging for their wares. For every programmer working to come up with new and better encryption or digital watermarking, there is someone on the other side working to circumvent the protection. In addition to the conflicting issues between content owners and consumers, there is another area of concern—the matter of fair use. Librarians are seeking to preserve the right to distribute limited numbers of copies of copyright works at no charge, as is acceptable with print.

Thus a delicate balance must be reached between the rightful claims of content owners, the legitimate use on the part of consumers, and the need to preserve fair use as put forth by librarians and other free speech advocates. The efforts to maintain the balance through the courts, through legislation, and through technological means will continue to evolve as technology itself becomes more sophisticated.

BIBLIOGRAPHY

Hamilton, A. (2002). "The Pirates of Prime Time." *Time* 159 (February 25), pp. 54-56.
Munro, N. and Clark, D. (2001). "Digital Dilemma." *National Journal* 33 (July 28), pp. 2386-2392.

Cybercafés

During the 1990s restaurants and coffeehouses offering Internet access sprang up around the world. The attraction was Internet access for visitors, offered in congenial settings along with food and beverages. Sometimes other services have been offered as well, as with a combination coffeehouse, Laundromat, and cybercafé in San Francisco. Typically a cybercafé offers an hourly rate for access and caters to people who find themselves without other convenient Internet access. Some establishments even offer brief tutorials for novices. Students, travelers, commuters, and others needing convenient access are likely patrons, with many businesses offering twenty-four-hour daily service. Customers name convenience as a strong draw in using cybercafés, but also report enjoying the atmosphere and other amenities.

The cybercafé concept has also been adapted by diverse venues that offer Internet access along with other services. Thus malls, hotels, auto rental agencies, and airports may provide kiosks with online access. Airlines, already aware of the popularity of telephone access, are making Internet access available to passengers as well. Copy centers such as Kinko's offer online access along with numerous other computer services and conveniences.

Cybercafés are especially popular in countries where other means of access are hard to come by. In developing countries, residents as well as travelers may find them to be the only places to gain Internet access. In countries such as China, students frequent cybercafés because their school access is often limited to their native language. Unfortunately, in some countries cybercafés are closing due to repression. Iran, Saudi Arabia, South Korea, Tunisia, and others have restricted Internet access in recent years. Despite restrictions, existing cybercafés in these and other countries around the world are exceedingly popular, even more so than in the United States, where Internet access is available in many environments.

BIBLIOGRAPHY

Gruenwald, J. (2001). "Cybercafe Crackdown." *Interactive Week* 8 (August 13), pp. 43-44.

McLaughlin, J. (1996). "Internet Cafes, Niche Marketing." *Restaurant Business* 95 (May 1), p. 98.

Whatis.com (2002). "Cybercafe." In *Whatis?com's Encyclopedia of Technology Terms*. Indianapolis, IN: Que.

Cyberspace

Cyberspace is a term coined by William Gibson in his 1984 novel *Neuromancer,* a work about a computer hacker ("Cowboy") riding along the "information-space." In an alternative future, economic and political power have been transformed into huge databases that are located in a structural manifold called the matrix or cyberspace,

> bright lattices of logic unfolding across that colorless void. The virtuosi of the matrix can experience cyberspace through electrodes attached to their foreheads and manipulate its structures through a keyboard computer called a deck. Cowboy operated on an almost permanent adrenaline high, a by-product of youth and proficiency, jacked into a custom cyberspace deck that projected his disembodied consciousness into the matrix.

Cyberspace, simply, is the global computer network, i.e., the Internet.

To begin, the Internet works not unlike a train system. Information is sent along cables, wire, satellite, and telephone lines in packets. A packet is a unit of data that travels across a network. When you send e-mail, download files, or pull up pages on your browser over the Internet, the information is sent and arrives in smaller packets rather than the entire file. Using the train model, every car is a packet and every Internet connection is a track. When the train leaves for its destination, it is coupled. However, as it travels, many of the cars split up and follow other tracks—all heading for the final destination. The train is then re-coupled, in proper order, at the destination—your machine. Packets were designed this way to speed up information travel. Packets, like train cars, actually split up after being sent, each traveling down a different track until the cars meet up, in order, on the other end of the line. This is quite fast as electronic information is made up of electrons that travel at the speed of light. However, as traffic and information packet size increase, the speed decreases. Traffic is always an issue. Packet size is an issue as well; increasingly so because information in the medium of audio/video is quite immense. At times, the current technology cannot keep up with the size of the information packets sent and received.

Millions of people are connected to each other through computers, allowing communication and sharing in a way that makes cyberspace an actual, albeit electronic, place.

BIBLIOGRAPHY

Gibson, W. (1984). *Neuromancer*. New York: Ace Books.

Cybersquatting/Domain Hijacking

Throughout history territorial disputes have led to countless altercations ranging from arguments between neighbors to global wars. Today the same sorts of problems proliferate in cyberspace. As the number of Internet addresses has mushroomed over the years, so have conflicts over the use of domain names and Web addresses. Problems have escalated to the extent that the federal government stepped in with the Anticybersquatting Consumer Protection Act of 1999, or ACPA, which seeks to protect trademark owners. Inventive cybersquatters carry out their nefarious deeds in several ways. If an entity registers a domain, achieves recognition for that legitimate site, and then fails to renew the registration, squatters often jump in and register the name for themselves. That is usually the reason why a computer user may correctly key in a URL, or return to a previously marked site, only to find pornographic or otherwise unwanted pages displayed. Another trick is to deliberately misspell someone else's address, using an approximation so close as to draw in unwitting Web searchers. Changing the suffix or domain name of a well-known location is yet another common practice. The most famous example of this ploy is the infamous Whitehouse address in which whitehouse. com leads to a porn site when keyed in rather than the official whitehouse.gov address. To complicate this particular instance even more, whitehouse.org yields a satirical site which, while not as offensive as the pornographic location, is still not the destination intended by anyone seeking accurate information.

Domain name holders are increasingly protective of their addresses, paying close attention to maintaining their registrations. It is up to the holder rather than the registrar to make sure his or her address does not fall into someone else's hands. Legislation such as the ACPA will likely evolve as Internet use changes and cybersquatters develop new techniques for misleading the unwary.

BIBLIOGRAPHY

Harrison, A. (2000). "Nike Web Hijacking Sparks Finger-Pointing." *Computerworld* 34 (July 10), p. 21.

Isenberg, D. (2001). "Domain Name Games." *Internet World* 7 (May 1), p. 31.

Lifshitz, A. (2001). "Cybersquatting." *Harvard Journal on Legislation* 38 (Summer), pp. 539-549.

Cybrarian

Cybrarians administer online information environments that offer access to an assortment of resources and information services. While not necessarily traditional librarians, cybrarians specialize in online research and information retrieval and attempt to develop and organize collections and services into a useful and integrated environment. These environments are not single entities; rather, they allow many transparent linkages to other environments that provide universal access to information and document collections, including digital items that cannot be displayed or distributed on paper (i.e., audio and video). Cybrarians not only mediate between diverse and distributed information, but also the changing range of user communities. In this, a library is less known for its holdings than its access to networked online environments. Consequently, we can think in terms of one all-encompassing library where patrons have access all the time, everywhere, on any device.

With large collections of information we can exploit the structure and context of individual works and their interrelationships through indexing, classification, and retrieval methods. In this, the cybrarian's focus is on knowledge representation, to include: two-dimensional graphical representations that are utilized to give better and more easily accessible overviews of a collection of documents; effective human interface design, including text, graphic, video, and audio displays to allow better retrieval; evaluation techniques, including both traditional relevance assessments and research on new ways of measuring utility and dealing with uncertainty in system performance; distributed and collaborative systems, including information sharing and the administrative and economic complexity of shared systems, document description, and relevance defined in probabilistic terms; and natural language text analysis, including lexical, syntactic, semantic, and pragmatic considerations, but focusing on how natural language processing can improve text retrieval.

BIBLIOGRAPHY

Fox, E.A. (Ed.) (1993). *Source Book on Digital Libraries.* Blacksburg, VA: Virginia Tech.

Peters, T.A. (2000). "Introduction." *Library Trends* 49(2) (Fall), pp. 221-227.

Deep Web

The *deep Web* refers to static content, including nontextual materials, that is stored in databases accessible through the Web. This content includes telephone books, dictionary definitions, library collections, Web-based auctions, news, stock reports, audio files, video files, etc. The deep Web is like a digital library—an online information environment offering access to an assortment of resources and information services. However, the deep Web is largely inaccessible to search engines because its pages do not exist until they are created dynamically via queries from such programs as Microsoft Access, Oracle, SQL (structured query language), and IBM's DB2. This information is accessible only by query. The deep Web tends to be narrower, with deeper content than conventional sites, and is highly relevant to every information need. The deep Web is up to 550 times larger than the World Wide Web, and resides in topic-specific databases. One reason that search engines do not index the deep Web is that search technologies are limited in their capabilities despite their tremendous usefulness in helping searchers locate text documents on the Web. Another reason is that it is expensive for search engines to locate Web resources and maintain up-to-date indexes, and, thus, impractical to operate a comprehensive search engine. Search engines must also deal with unreliable information. Because practically everyone may post information to the Internet, it is highly likely that much of the information is incorrect, incomplete, or deceptive. The deep Web is the fastest-growing category of new information on the Internet. It has been asserted that the deep Web will be the dominant source of information for the next-generation Internet. The deep Web is sometimes referred to as the *Invisible Web*.

BIBLIOGRAPHY

Bergman, M.K. (2001). "The Deep Web: Surfacing Hidden Value." *The Journal of Electronic Publishing* (7)1. Available from <http://www.press.umich.edu/jep/07-01/bergman.html>.

Complete Planet.com (n.d.). "Help and FAQs." Available from <http://www.completeplanet.com/help/help_deepwebFAQs.asp>.

Sherman, C. and Price, G. (2001). *The Invisible Web: Uncovering Information Sources Search Engines Can't See.* CyberAge Books: Medford, NJ.

Digital Audio

Digital audio is the conversion of sound into binary digits, a process using positive and no positive states, represented by the numbers 1 and 0 respectively. This makes the sound more compressed and faster. "In order for users to receive sound in real-time for a multimedia effect, listening to music, or in order to take part in an audio conference, sound must be delivered as streaming sound" (Whatis?.com, 2002, p. 52).

Digital audio recording began in the 1970s with a project to store and retrieve video images. The project, initiated by Philips and later supported jointly by Philips and Sony, had many obstacles and soon the focus was shifted to sound recording. Philips and Sony produced the first commercial digital audio recording in 1979. The first commercially available compact disc (CD) player was manufactured four years later in 1983. Other than this enterprise, little attention was given to digital audio, and those who tried to market the format commercially seemed to fail with the public. One such failure was the Betamax digital audio tape.

It has only been in the past few years that interest in digital audio has grown. The compact disc was created to be used as a universal delivery medium for digitized music. The compact disc digital audio system uses the Red Book as its standard. Introduced in 1980 by Philips and Sony, the Red Book is named after a set of books containing the specifications for all CD formats. Companies now offer a variety of digital audio players, including CD/MP3 players. The use of CD/MP3 players and other similar products has quadrupled since 2000, and with new wireless technology the use of digital audio is predicted to quadruple again within the next three years. Many users can now use writable CDs, which are fairly inexpensive, to create their own music files.

Digital audio is closely linked to the computer. Audio cards allow people to use their computers as they once used radios. A new digital audio converter allows a user to set the level of sound. This converter keeps the volume at a consistent level regardless of interferences. This is great for those using audio in the workplace.

Since 2002 new products and services have been introduced that will introduce a new era for digital audio. Some of these products are peripherals for obtaining the best sound from the audio recording. One noted example are the newer, more sensitive, microphones that are being introduced in the digital broadcast market.

BIBLIOGRAPHY

Daley, D. (2001). "Digital Audio: Using Microphones." *World Broadcast Engineering* 24(11) (November), p. 12.

Institute of Electrical and Electronic Engineers (IEEE) (2003). "Going Digital: Digital Audio Recording." Available from <http://www.ieee.org/organizations/history_center/going_digital.html>.

Saracco, R., Harrow, J.R., and Weihmayer, R. (2000). *The Disappearance of Telecommunications.* New York: IEEE Press.

Smith, D. (2002). "Digital Voice: An Update and Forecast." *QST* 86 (February), pp. 38-41.

Whatis.com (n.d.). "Audio." Available from <http://whatis.techtarget.com/definition/0,,sid9_gci211617,00.html>.

Whatis.com (n.d.). "Digital." Available from <http://whatis.techtarget.com/definition/0,,sid9_gci211948,00.html>.

Wolf, C. (2002). "Growth Expected for All Portable Digital Audio Products." *Electronic News* (August 5), p. 12.

Digital Camera

A *digital camera* is a camera that records and then stores its images in a digital form. The images can then be loaded into a computer, where they can be manipulated in various ways. These cameras have a lens, aperture, and shutter, but do not use film.

The origins of the digital camera can be linked with the evolution of television in the 1950s. In the beginning television could only be broadcast live, and it was not until 1950, when Bing Crosby Laboratories introduced the video tape recorder (VTR), a technology specifically designed to record images, that these images could be captured. In the early 1960s, NASA decided it needed video cameras that could transmit signals from the moon. Researchers at NASA developed ways to enhance signals by processing them through computers, thus giving clearer images.

How does the digital camera work? It first captures an image through a charged coupling device (CCD), which converts the image into electrical impulses. A digital camera's resolution is the number of pixels on the CCD. The resolution determines the clarity of the image. The image is then fed into a microprocessor, where it is transformed into digital information. The image can then be viewed and manipulated.

In 1995 Kodak released the first digital cameras to the public. Color digital cameras have three different sensors to capture various colors and hues.

As with most technology, digital cameras have many uses. Several models of cellular telephones have digital cameras built into them that permit users to take, view, and electronically transmit photographs. In 2003, archaeologists lowered a digital camera into a Zapotec tomb in El Palmillo, Mexico, allowing them to view the tomb's contents without having to disturb the area (Dellios, 2003).

BIBLIOGRAPHY

Bellis, M. (n.d.). "History of the Digital Camera." Available from <http://inventors. about.com/library/inventors/bldigitalcamera.htm>.

Biedermann, B. (2001). "A Camera in Every Cell Phone Could Be Just Around the Corner." *Electronic Design* 49(22) (October 29), p. 34.

Dellios, H. "Archaeologists Stumble Upon Tomb of Ancient Mexican Civilization." *Chicago Tribune* (July 8), p. 6.

Sony-digitalcamera.com (n.d.). "History of the Digital Camera." Available from <http://www.sony-digitalcamera.com/history.html>.

Whatis.com (n.d.). "Digital Camera." Available from <http://whatis.techtarget. com/definition/0,,sid9_gci211950,00.html>.

Digital Cinema

From 1829, when Louis-Jaques-Mandé Dauguerre joined with Joseph-Nicéphore Niepce to pursue photographic inventions, to 1877, when Thomas Edison recorded sound onto a cylinder, the film industry had its beginnings. It was not until 1895 that the first portable camera was developed, which Edison quickly used and demonstrated his first motion picture in public the next year. Then in 1900 a strike by vaudeville performers caused theater owners to present all-film programs. These proved to be hugely popular. Soon movie theaters began springing up all over. Another breakthrough came in 1912 when motorized movie cameras replaced hand cranks. Despite many ups and downs, films continued to be made with various modifications until 1992, when the first public demonstration of digital cinema was shown. The coverage of digital cinema garnered more attention than the film itself. It was not until 1999 that digital cinema demonstrations to the general public began. Lucas Films and 20th-Century Fox debuted *Star Wars: Episode 1—The Phantom Menace* as the first major motion picture theatrically exhibited as digital cinema. As of 2002 there are more than forty digital cinema theaters in the world, and seven major motion picture studios have formed a company, Digital Cinema Initiatives (formerly NewCo Digital Cinema), to set new standards for digital cinema.

But what is digital cinema? From the beginning cinema was defined as "the art of motion." The first images were created and animated manually. Devices that could animate more than just a few images became more popular. These devices, such as the Zootrope, were based on loops. Edison's Kinetoscope, the first modern cinematic machine to employ film, used this technique. Then digitalizing took place. Now scenes can be generated in a computer with the help of 3-D computer animation. Live-action footage can be digitalized. Any method used to create an image can be captured using pixels. Pixels can then be manipulated to create illusions. This is how films such as *Toy Story* were created. Thus digital film equals live-action material plus painting plus image processing plus compositing plus 2-D animation plus 3-D animation. The latest in digital cinema is high-definition video (HDV), which can record video and audio and still be used with the VCR format.

With the dawning of the twenty-first century, the field of digital cinema is wide open. One author stated that if we thought the progress made in the past ten years has been astonishing, just wait. These will seem like the dark ages compared to what will be developed within the next ten years. Today's accomplishments are only the beginning.

BIBLIOGRAPHY

Mendrala, J. (2002). "A Brief History of Film and Digital Cinema." Available from <http://www.tech-notes.tv/Dig-Cine/Digitalcinema.html>.

Shatkin, Elina (2003). "New HDV Format Proposed." (August 13). Available from <http://www.uemedia.com/CPC/article_11136.shtml>.

Wyatt, R.B. (1998). "Welcome to Digital Cinema Today." Available from <http://tech-head.com/cinema.htm>.

Digital Imaging

Digital imaging is closely tied with the development of digital cameras and the television. It's based on the idea that an image can be turned into electrical patterns that can be digitized, or turned into computer binary code. Once the image has been translated into computer language, it can be manipulated in ways that are limited only by the imagination of the user. Digital imaging can make the dead walk, or so it seems. For example, photos of Abraham Lincoln can be digitized and animated, giving the images the illusion of life. It is at its best when it produces images that enhance the understanding and facilitate the interpretation of large, complicated data sets. Imaging was originally produced by photomechanical means. This was a lengthy and complex method that was also costly. Later, drum scanners were developed, which cut the time and cost to produce the images. Then, in the 1970s, microprocessors were created that could take the signal from a photo multiplier tube and store it in a computer in which the images could be manipulated. These processes were very expensive. It was not until desktop computers, laser printers, and the PostScript computer language came in the late 1970s that digital imaging was made more affordable. Today it is increasingly found in our "everyday" lives.

Imaging technologies have contributed to virtually all areas of science. It has applications from interactive video games, film, and television special effects/graphics/animation, manufacturing for visualizing computer assisted design data, forensic and legal reconstructions, to probably one of its greatest usages, medicine, especially in the area of CT scans. The use of these images is safer for the patient and will contribute to a healthier person as more medical imaging clinics are being built. These clinics use the imaging technique to view the human body without being invasive. This use alone has been worth the efforts of all who made digital imaging possible.

This 1985 picture shows digital imaging already in use for medical treatment. The woman pictured had joint replacement surgery. (*Source: Infonautics in the U.S.A.* 53 (1985). Washington, DC: The United States Information Agency.)

BIBLIOGRAPHY

Bertrand, C.A. (2001). "Color by Number: Imaging Large Data." *Science* 293(5533) (August 17), p. 1335.

Morgan Rockhill PhotoDigital, Inc. (n.d.). "A Brief History of Digital Imaging." Available from <http://www.pixelphoto.com/htdocs/html/history.html>.

O'Reilly, E. (2001). *Making Career Sense of Labour Market Information.* Ottawa: Canadian Career Development Foundation. Available from <http://makingcareersense. org>.

Digital Video

According to Dadgar (1999), a *digital video* is "video that is recorded digitally. It is the combination of sound and pictures that are manipulated by a computer to generate digital images. Digital video is the computer data that represents these images" (p. 1). It can also integrate visual and auditory information for a very effective presentation. What makes it different from other formats is that it encodes a signal that filters out noise, which was always a big problem in analog formats.

The history of digital video can be said to have begun with the invention of the telephone and later with the phonograph and radio. Digital computers first became available after World War II, but it was not until the 1960s, when integrated circuits brought costs down, that they became affordable to many consumers. With the merger of technology in the computer and television field, the ability to produce interactive digital video became a reality. Digital video is versatile, easily stored, and cheap. The quality stays the same over time. As White (2000) states, "The days of peering at a jerky, squashed-down distortion of a video clip are quickly drawing to a close" (p. 4). Digital video also can store a large amount of data, and with the ability to integrate audio one can add any number of special effects.

Digital video camcorders got a boost for the average consumer when Sony introduced the DV format allowing easy connectivity to a computer. The quality of the material was such that most users felt they were producing professional videos. Wyatt (1998) felt that the current state of digital technology is more than adequate to meet the challenges of streaming video internationally and almost in real time.

BIBLIOGRAPHY

Dadgar, S. (1999). "Overview of Digital Video." Available from <http://et.sdsu.edu/sphares/videoWebpage/history.htm>.

Ozer, J. (2003). "Make Digital Videos Worth Watching." *PC Magazine* 22 (14), p. 62.

PCTechGuide.com (2003). "Multimedia/Digital Video: History." Available from <http://www.pctechguide.com/24digvid.htm>.

White, C. (2002). "The Digital Video Divide." Available from <http://production. digitalmedianet.com/2002/03_mar/editorials/cw_editorial462.htm>.

White, R. (2000). "A Brief Personal History of Digital Video: Do Good Things Really Come in Small Packages?" Available from <http://www.aila.artinstitutes. edu/dj/docs/digitalvideo_1.htm>.

Wyatt, R.B. (1998). "Global Webcasting with Streaming Video." *Videomaker* (September), pp. 130-133.

Distance Learning

Distance learning has its roots in correspondence education conducted via mail. The student "corresponds" with the school in sending and receiving assignments, tests, and lessons. This method of education has been used in the United States for almost a century. Since the advent of information technologies, cable, satellite, wireless telecommunications, personal computers, and the Internet, a transformation of distance learning has taken place. For many world citizens, the services, content, and instant expertise available through these technologies is offered as an alternative to overpriced international telephone and postal services, and in a way that is not readily available locally. Issues of time, space, and geography are no longer hindrances for diverse populations to participate in higher education.

While distance learning takes a wide variety of forms, it may be characterized as a separation of place and/or time between the professor and students, and the interaction through one or more media technologies. Online classes are typically the most popular because of the convenience of being able to do research and other correspondence over the Internet, utilizing tools by which the participants already have access.

Technology augments distance learning. Distance learners utilizing these technologies are allowed an increased access to advanced or specialized classes.

BIBLIOGRAPHY

Cairncross, F. (1997). *The Death of Distance: How the Communications Revolution Will Change Our Lives*. Boston, MA: Harvard Business School Press.

Mood, T.A. (1995). *Distance Education: An Annotated Bibliography*. Englewood, CO: Libraries Unlimited, Inc.

Domains

As the number of Internet sites grew exponentially along with the growth of the World Wide Web, finding specific locations became accordingly more challenging. URLs, or uniform resource locators, were developed to serve as Internet addresses and facilitate location of information. A URL contains a descriptor, or series of descriptors of a given location, followed by a suffix. The suffix, or domain, is set apart by a period followed by a standardized abbreviation that denotes its nature. The domain is that part of an Internet address that denotes the nature of the entity that posted the site. The most famous and largest domain is the ubiquitous ".com". The domain name suffix, known as the top-level domain or TLD, serves as a vital indicator in a URL. The number of TLDs is limited, with their adoptions determined by the Internet Corporation for Assigned Names and Numbers, or ICANN. Prior to 2000, the accepted top-level domains were the following:

.gov—Government agencies
.edu—Educational institutions
.org—Organizations (nonprofit)
.mil—Military
.com—Commercial business
.net—Network organizations

Countries could also have domains such as the following:

.ca—Canada
.au—Australia
.uk—Great Britain

As of 2000, Icann approved seven new top-level domains to augment the original list. These TLDs included the following:

.biz—Business
.info—Unrestricted (open to any use)
.name—Individuals
.pro—Accountants, lawyers, physicians, and other professions
.museum—Museums
.aero—Air transport industry
.coop—cooperatives

While "dot-com" has become a cliché, it is clear that the designators now called TLDs are influential in bringing order to the myriad number of Internet sites on the World Wide Web. Whether the current presentation of TLDs is sufficient or more may need to be designated in the future remains to be seen.

BIBLIOGRAPHY

ICANN (n.d.). *ICANN: The Internet Corporation for Assigned Names and Numbers.* Available from <http://www.icann.org/>.
Isenberg, D. (2001). "Domain Name Games." *Internet World* 7 (May 1), p. 31.

Dot-Com

Dot-com was specifically intended as a term for a business site; however, in some cases it has become a general term for any Web site. The term *com* is the form that completes the last part for most commercial Web sites. It is the address, the "dot address," that refers to the notation that expresses the four-byte (32-bit) IP address as a sequence of four decimal numbers separated by dots. For example, to learn the dot address (such as 205.245.172.72) for a given domain name, Windows users can go to their MS DOS prompt screen and enter: ping xxx.yyy where "xxx" is the second-level domain name, such as "whatis", and ".yyy" is the top-level domain name, such as ".com"). The separation of the four numbers with dots makes the address easier to read. Of course, most of us remember an Internet location by its domain name rather than its numbered Internet address. However, we sometimes need the dot address when we configure a Web browser or activate an account with an Internet service provider.

As the stock market began to decline in the late 1990s, *dot-com* became synonymous with a number of failed Web businesses. The open standards of the Internet, which make it easy for new businesses to enter the market, are also a great weakness. Many businesses and investors rallied behind the dot-coms thinking they would make lots of money. This appeared to be the case when Internet stock prices rose sharply in the early 1990s. Amazon.com's stock, for example, increased 966 percent in value from its initial entry into the market. However, with the decline of the stock market, many companies lost millions of dollars. Even those Internet companies that continue to operate have lower profit margins than traditional companies offering similar goods or services.

The number of Internet sites grew so fast it became necessary to have a way to distinguish different entities; thus, in addition to dot-com, dot-org, dot-gov, and dot-edu were used.

BIBLIOGRAPHY

Cairncross, F. (2001). *The Death of Distance: How the Communications Revolution Is Changing Our Lives.* Boston, MA: Harvard Business School Press.

Whatis.com (2002). "Dot Com." *Whatis?com's Encyclopedia of Technology Terms.* Indianapolis, IN: Que.

Early Adopters

The term *early adopters* refers to eager users of technology who have the interest and financial wherewithal to buy new products as soon as they appear on the market. They don't wait for manufacturers to work out all the kinks, or for prices to go down. They are driven to be the first to own and show off new gadgets and devices. In his book *The Invisible Computer,* Donald Norman (1998) credits early adopters with being the key to the advancement of new technologies. Someone has to go first and give new devices a chance before they can gain wide recognition and distribution. Early adopters tend to be affluent, a necessary attribute that allows them the means to buy new items that they find appealing. Manufacturers of devices such as digital cameras, digital music players, PDAs, and other gadgets need early purchasers to get their products off the ground. Detractors may say that wasteful buying habits fuel the fire as more and more gizmos of questionable value glut the market, but promoters of new products pin their hopes on them. The adventurous early adopters may lose money by buying early and find themselves wanting upgrades of items early in the game, but these are risks they knowingly and willingly take. Their initiatives help make it possible for everyone else to enjoy new products a little later, after they have been perfected and affordably priced.

BIBLIOGRAPHY

Coates, J. (2002). "'Early Adopters' Hold Key to New Technologies." *Chicago Tribune* (April 17), p. 4.

Norman, D. (1998). *The Invisible Computer.* Cambridge, MA: MIT Press.

Easter Eggs

Many Americans have fond memories of searching for hidden eggs during Easter season. The desires to hide and search for treasure are the motivators behind computer Easter eggs. Easter eggs are generally harmless messages or software included inside other computer programs. These fun and entertaining tidbits are commonly hidden by software creators in the products they develop. Literally thousands of these little surprises are hidden in various applications. An early and popular example is the flight simulator game hidden in Microsoft Excel 97. This game could be accessed by following a simple series of steps that involved opening a new worksheet, going to an assigned cell, formatting it as prescribed, and clicking Control/Shift. For a long time this game was a favorite of students who were apt to play it instead of pursuing more productive activities during class time.

Easter eggs can also be found in DVDs. As with other computer applications, they are hidden where only the knowledgeable user can locate them, usually by hitting key combinations on the remote control. Hidden surprises may include scenes that did not make it into the final movie, outtakes, musical additions, and interviews with cast members. As with other applications, the secrets to accessing DVD Easter eggs are offered via Internet pages such as *The Easter Egg Archive* (http://www.eeggs.com), *DVD Review* (http://www.dvdreview.com) and *DVD* (http://dvd.ign.com). Old as well as new productions may offer surprises, such as the DVD of *Dr. No,* which offers a history of the martini, James Bond's favorite beverage.

Some eggs are very simple, such as pictures of the development team for a particular application. Others can be much more complex and, while considered fun by some users, are denounced by others for taking up memory, bloating computer codes, and for being included without telling the purchaser. In some cases they have been known to present content or images that might be objectionable to some users. Software manufacturers often go to great lengths to discourage the inclusion of Easter eggs, and developers continually try to rise to the challenge of slipping them by security and quality control measures. The fact that they slip by may be a reflection of poor quality control on the part of some manufacturers, which is another concern.

Keeping up with eggs can be fun, and one of the best ways to find them is by doing a Net search for "Easter eggs." These sites are updated regularly, invite contributions from visitors, and often rate the eggs as well as tell users how to find them.

BIBLIOGRAPHY

DVD. Available from <http://dvd.ign.com/>.
DVD Review. Available from <http://www.dvdreview.com/>.
The Easter Egg Archive (n.d.). Available from <http://www.eeggs.com>.
"Hidden 'Easter Eggs' Can Brighten DVD Movies." *Denver Rocky Mountain News* (November 30, 2001), p. 3D. Available from <http://www.bigchalk.com>.
Russell, K. (2000). "Easter Eggs." *Computerworld* 34 (September 18), p. 74.

E-Books

An *e-book* is an electronic presentation of a conventional print book that is available online and can be read with a computer, e-book reader, or PDA (personal digital assistant). Readers turn to e-books for convenience and portability. The term *e-book* has several spellings, including Ebook and eBook. Adding to the confusion, some people refer to e-books as the actual text files or unencrypted HTML, whereas others use the term in reference to the reading device. Thus the term has been used to refer to hardware and software, as well as documents.

Publishing companies are debating the issue of making books available in electronic format. Most want to charge fees for downloads, since the book must be scanned or typed in. Electronic textbooks offer the advantage of continuous updating, shortening the publishing cycles of materials. To maintain their competitive edge, publishers will need to keep pace in order to meet the growing need for information via e-books.

Most students today are accustomed to obtaining information instantly, therefore e-books will fit easily into this Internet age. Books are quickly becoming electronic bits, and those bits provide access to knowledge as never before. Scores of people who could never before obtain access to certain kinds of ancient and rare books now can access them electronically. This increased availability calls for new types of librarians, journalists, and publishers. The printed word is now easily accessed via computer, thus changing the way professionals must deal with information. The new media will eventually change peoples' expectations just as printed books once did.

BIBLIOGRAPHY

"E-Books." (2000). *Whatis?com's Encyclopedia of Technology Terms.* Indianapolis: Que, p. 220.

Saracco, R., Harrow, J.R., and Weihmayer, R. (2000). *The Disappearance of Tele-communications.* New York: IEEE Press.

"What are eBooks?" (2000). Available from <http://www.electricstory.com/about_ebooks.asp>.

"What is an eBook?" (2003). Available from <http://www.chartula.com/ebookdef.htm>.

Wilson, R. (2002). "The Problem of Defining Electronic Books." Available from <http://ebooks.strath.ac.uk/eboni/documents/definition.html>.

Electronic Publishing

Electronic publishing has been defined as the application of computers to primarily "front end" the publishing process. This definition may have been a facetious attempt to explain how electronic publishing actually began with the use of the computer. Many define it as producing documents to be viewed on a computer screen that may never be printed on paper. In addition to Internet and World Wide Web, many CD-ROM products have answered the demands to "go electronic." Electronic publishing may include video and sound clips, animated graphics, and even links. These materials may be original or they may have been paper published and then transferred to electronic format.

Electronic publishing has undergone several phases. It began as text e-mail in the 1980s. The first electronic journal was published in the early 1990s. E-journal distribution began in the mid-1990s, and many online journals included hypertext links and other multimedia tools. Electronic publishers did not realize how popular this medium would be. To meet demand, many publishers "jumped before they looked" and soon found themselves adrift without the needed guidelines. "How hard could it be to publish something electronically?" they asked. Several things had not been considered. Most found it took longer than they had anticipated; it was more labor intensive than first thought; and, more important, it cost more than they had anticipated. At first many were trying to publish in both formats, meaning print and electronically, which added to the cost. The demand was also there for links, animation, etc., which also added to the cost.

In 2001 several companies, Cox Enterprises, ESPN.com, Knight Ridder Digital, and New York Times Digital, came together to establish The Online Publishers Association, which was formed to represent the interests of high-quality digital publishers. Because the Internet is global, there needs to be publishing models for Internet commerce, and the print publishing market could provide some of the best models for the commercial Internet. A variety of new tools for publishing on the Internet are being developed, and when standard-ization can be maintained, all consumers will benefit.

BIBLIOGRAPHY

"Electronic Publishing." (2003). *Computer User.Com Magazine.* Available from <http://www.computeruser.com/resources/dictionary/definition.html>.

Pack, T. (2001). "Online Publishers Association Formed." *EContent* 24(7) (September), p. 9.

Pettenati, C. (2001). "Electronic Publishing at the End of 2001." Available from <http://nss2000.mi.infn.it/Manuscripts/10_generalities/pettenati.pdf>, pp. 1-9.

E-Mail

E-mail, or electronic mail, is the exchange or transmission of computer-stored messages by telecommunications. E-mail was one of the first uses of the Internet and still remains the most popular use. It is particularly beneficial in areas without land lines. With e-mail, even those who live in the most rural areas can have access to the same information as those who live in the city. Sent messages are stored in electronic mailboxes until the recipient opens the e-mail. All online services and Internet service providers (ISPs) offer e-mail.

New mobile communication and e-mail have indeed made the world, the universe, a much smaller and more accessible place. That, again, is the purpose and first great use of the Internet—people reaching people. Although versions of e-mail date back to the 1960s, the first e-mail was sent in 1970, and similar to the first wire communication, it was astonishing. Ray Tomlinson, who is credited for developing the first e-mail application, reportedly told a colleague, "Don't tell anyone! This isn't what we're supposed to be working on." Tomlinson is also credited for his decision to use the @ symbol as the locator sign in e-mail. For detailed information about Tomlinson's story go to <http://www.pretext.com/mar98/features/story2.htm>.

E-mail is accessible because it is low tech—no fancy software or other gadgets are needed. It is also very cheap. One can keep in touch via e-mail for less than it costs to send a postcard or make a phone call from any part of the world. E-mail is also very flexible. It allows articles, pictures, or even songs to be sent with just a click of the mouse. It has been estimated that 3 trillion e-mails are sent daily in the United States.

E-mail is composed of an e-mail address, which must be entered correctly if the intended recipient is to be reached, a subject line, which good netiquette calls for one to enter to let the recipient know what the e-mail is about, and the message. Most e-mail messages are informal and brief. After composing the message, the e-mail is sent by clicking on an icon or the word "send." However, it is a good idea to reread your message and do a spell check before sending the e-mail. A message may also contain an attachment. These attachments may be photos, images, or other media.

E-mail has found a place in the voice of the citizenry. Citizens are able to ascertain a politician's view and e-mail their own opinions to the politician. It was reported that former president Bill Clinton received 2,000 e-mails daily while he was in office.

BIBLIOGRAPHY

Cairncross, F. (2001). *The Death of Distance: How the Communications Revolution Is Changing Our Lives.* Boston, MA: Harvard Business School Press.

Campbell, T. (1998). "The First E-Mail Message: Who Sent it and What it Said." Available at <http://www.pretext.com/mar98/features/story2.htm>.

Crocker, D. (2003). "Email History." Available at <http://livinginternet.com/?e/ei. htm>.

Webopedia.com (n.d.). "E-mail." Available at <http://www.webopedia.com/TERM/E/ e_mail.html>.

Whatis.com (2002). "E-mail." *Whatis?com's Encyclopedia of Technology Terms.* Indianapolis, IN: Que, p. 233. Available at <http://searchNetworking.techtarget. com/sDefinition/0,,sid7_gci212051,00.html>.

Emoticons

Internet e-mail and chat have the disadvantages of not allowing users to adequately express emotions. Someone can make a statement in jest, or with an ironic intent, and have it taken at face value. To help alleviate this problem, emoticons have evolved. The term *emoticon* is short for emotion icon. Combinations of punctuation marks, numbers, and letters, usually viewed sideways, are used to help express a writer's mood. The most famous emoticon of all is the basic "smiley", or ":-)". Other facial expressions followed the smiley, including the "frowny", "wink", and "crying face". Creative inventions abound with endless possibilities.

The history of emoticons goes all the way back to the earliest communication exchanges via ARPANET. As early as 1979, the idea emerged to use punctuation marks to denote emotions, such as "-)" to suggest "tongue-in-cheek." As Usenet groups became popular in the 1980s, emoticons continued to evolve and increase in popularity. One widely recognized symbol, the "frowny", ":-(", even gained trademark status in May 2000 when Dallas-based Despair, Inc., had it officially registered. Despair, Inc., sells items such as posters, greeting cards, mugs, and other promotional items that spoof the popular motivational products often seen in offices and schools. After obtaining the legitimate trademark, Despair, Inc.'s CEO, Dr. E. L. Kersten, proceeded to offer frownies for sale for the price of $0.00 each, a publicity stunt that helped gain recognition for the company's other products.

Users are encouraged to use these devices to minimize confusion when communicating electronically. Some common examples include:

;-)	Wink	:'-(	Crying
:-o	Shouting	<:-I	Dunce
:-/	Perplexed	>:-	Angry
(*)	Hug and kiss		

BIBLIOGRAPHY

Park, K. (2001). "Internet Lingo." *World Almanac and Book of Facts, 2001.* New York: World Almanac Books.

Russell, K. (2002). "Emoticons and Internet Shorthand." *Computerworld* 36 (January 14), p. 42.

Whatis.com (2001). "Emoticons." *Whatis?com's Encyclopedia of Technology Terms.* Indianapolis, IN: Que.

ENIAC

Desperate times are the mother of invention. War, or impending war in particular, has spurred many scientific advances—from the atomic bomb and space rockets to the computer. With World War II on the horizon, the U.S. Army's Ordnance Department began to test its weapons in the late 1930s. One critical task was the preparation of bombing and firing tables, which fell to the Ballistics Research Laboratory at Aberdeen Proving Grounds in Maryland. The laboratory was assisted in its computational efforts by a device known as the Bush Differential Analyzer (BDA)—a continuous variable calculator. Unfortunately, the Army's analyzer broke frequently, and a contract was awarded to the University of Pennsylvania for use of its BDA, which was more reliable and capable of making larger computations.

In June 1943, a second contract was awarded to the University of Pennsylvania for development of an "electronic numerical integrator and computer" (ENIAC). Designed by John Mauchly and J. Presper Eckert, ENIAC weighed a monstrous thirty tons and occupied 16,200 square feet. Its main elements included 19,000 vacuum tubes, which were spread among eight basic circuit components. An IBM card was used for inputting data, and a cardpunch was used for output. The machine was completed and shown to the public on February 15, 1946. Powerful for its time, ENIAC could perform 5,000 additions and 300 multiplications per second. It was accurate and did not break down as often as expected. One problem encountered with the machine was the amount of heat it generated. Fortunately, its designers had the foresight to install wheels on its components, and the machine was moved to an air-cooled room. Another problem with ENIAC was that its vacuum tubes often burned out, which required that the affected component be shut down during replacement.

In 1947, ENIAC was put to work at Aberdeen, where it remained operational until its permanent shutdown in 1955. During its years of service, ENIAC was used for weather predictions, cosmic-ray stud-

Following their success with ENIAC, Eckert and Mauchly created a more sophisticated computer called UNIVAC. In this 1959 picture, one man observes another as the computer is set up to predict the winner of a horse race. (*Source:* Hiller, H. "One Man Looks On . . ." *World Telegram and Sun* (1959). From Washington, DC: Library of Congress Prints and Photographs Collection.)

ies, wind-tunnel design, and atomic-energy calculations, in addition to ballistics computation. Today, several of ENIAC's designs and components are on display at the University of Pennsylvania, as well as the Smithsonian and other museums around the world.

BIBLIOGRAPHY

Goldschmidt, A. and Akera, A. (2003). "John W. Mauchly and the Development of the ENIAC Computer." Available from <www.library.upenn.edu/exhibits/rbm/mauchly/jwmintro.html>.

Richey, K. (1997). "The ENIAC." Available from <http://ei.cs.vt.edu/~history/ENIAC.Richey.HTML>.

Weik, M. (1961). "The ENIAC Story." *The Journal of the American Ordnance Association* January-February, pp. 3-7.

Winegrad, D. and Akera, A. (1996). "A Short History of the Second American Revolution." Available from <http://www.upenn.edu/almanac/v42/n18/eniac.html>.

E-Zines

E-zines, or electronic magazines, are increasingly popular Internet resources. They range from amateur to professional productions, with subject offerings from pop culture to scholarly pursuits. In some cases a publication may exist in digital format only. Others may be electronic versions of print magazines. Often they are free, supported by advertising, although some charge for subscriptions.

In most cases, even when an e-zine is related to a print magazine or journal, it is not an exact replication. Photo rights and other restrictions may result in some things being offered in print, but absent online. A free online version of a print journal often offers readers selected articles, directing them to the hard copy for additional content. Web journalists are increasingly aware that the differences in the two formats, print versus digital, call for different presentation styles. Online journals are more likely to attract users wanting an interactive experience, while the print format is more conducive to reading lengthy text passages.

Will e-zines replace print magazines and journals? One barrier is the lack of profit. Internet consumers are not accustomed to and do not want to pay for online information. Only if that mindset were to change would digital be likely to completely replace print for an established publication, especially in view of the fact that publishing online can be very expensive. Furthermore, the online experience differs from the experience of using a print publication. According to Louise Bishop (1998), online publications tend to offer more immediate connectivity to readers, often being updated daily. They also tend to be more visual, depending on graphics for communication rather than prose. Print publications, while also using graphics, tend to appeal to readers wanting longer prose offerings. Because of these differences, both formats may well enjoy continuing demand.

BIBLIOGRAPHY

Bishop, L. (1998). "Form vs. Function." *Creative Review* (April), pp. 16-18.
Weisser, C. (2000). "E-zine Lessons." *Internet World* 6 (December 15), p. 30.
Whatis.com (2001). "Ezines." *Whatis?com's Encyclopedia of Technology Terms.*
    Indianapolis, IN: Que.

Filtering

The World Wide Web presents a vast sea of information. Since the Internet first came online in late 1969, the number of users has grown to more than 600 million worldwide. The challenge facing the user is to find the best possible resources to meet his or her specific needs. An added complication is the fact that some of what is offered via the Internet can be less than authoritative, offensive, or even dangerous, and regulations that govern other resources are lacking. This is a matter of particular concern to adults who are worried about the access children may gain to pornography, hate materials, or just plain erroneous information. One solution to this dilemma has been information filtering devices. Strictly speaking, an Internet filter is an application that accepts information as input and changes or transforms it to meet certain specifications.

Because of their ability to block out certain material, filtering devices have become attractive to those who wish to restrict Internet access to children. In 2001 Congress passed the Children's Internet Protection Act, or CIPA. This policy required public schools to employ technology that blocks or filters Internet access to materials that are obscene or harmful to minors. Such software was to be in place by July 2002 in order for schools to receive federal technology funding. Also passed was the Neighborhood Children's Internet Protection Act, which required that school Internet safety policies extend to e-mail, hacking, chat rooms, and use or distribution of personal information about minors.

While the intentions behind Internet filtering are laudable, in practice the use of filtering software brings about a number of problems. Sites that are valid and useful may be rendered inaccessible, whereas harmful sites may pass through the filter. For example, Internet sites that offer information about a number of health and social issues are frequently blocked. The best available software is reported to be about 85 percent successful. At the same time, adults who should be supervising children's Internet use, whether at school or at home, may be lulled into a false sense of security by the presence of filters, and thus exercise inadequate personal supervision. Further, there are many ways to get around filtering software, which are well within the range of expertise of young users. Finally, although filters may block sites that are inappropriate, they never claim to restrict access to poorly presented, poorly researched, or even fallacious information that students may encounter.

The American Library Association filed a lawsuit in 2000 objecting to CIPA on the grounds that it was an unconstitutional restriction to full and free access to information. In June 2000 a three-judge panel in Philadelphia issued an injunction stating that, although CIPA could continue in public school libraries, it could not be enforced in public libraries because it violated First Amendment rights. In June 2003, the issue was revisited, and the Supreme Court reversed the Philadelphia ruling. In a 6 to 3 vote, the requirement that public libraries as well as school libraries add filters in order to receive federal funding was approved. Since then some public libraries, such as the San Francisco Public Library, have decided to forego federal funds rather than add filters. The cost of software to perform the blocking, along with technical staffing costs are factors influencing such a decision. The additional concern that filtering limits patrons' access to information is also a major concern.

BIBLIOGRAPHY

Bocher, B. (2003). "A CIPA Toolkit." *Library Journal* 128 (August), pp. 36-37.

Borja, R. (2002). "Internet Filtering Is Balancing Act for Many Schools." *Education Week* 21 (January 16), pp. 1-2.

"Court Overturns CIPA: Government Will Appeal." (2002). *American Libraries* 33 (August), pp. 18-20.

D'Arcy, J. (1999). "Policing the Web." *Macleans* 112 (September 13), pp. 14+.

"NUA Internet: How Many Online." (2002). Available from <http://www.nua.ie/surveys/how_many_online/>.

Gaming

Using a computer as a game station is nothing new. In 1958, Willy Higginbotham, head of the Instrumentation Division at Brookhaven National Laboratory, conducted tours to show the public what Brookhaven was up to and how safe the research laboratories were. Higginbotham wanted to show more than pictures and slide shows. He connected a computer to an oscilloscope with a small five-inch screen, added resistors, capacitors, vacuum tubes, and other circuitry to compute wind speed, gravity, and bounce to display a ball on the screen. He also used an upside-down T drawn on the screen to represent a net. Visitors were now able to see and try a hands-on video game—tennis. Higginbotham also built controllers out of blocks of wood with a button and dial mounted. The button was used to hit the ball and the dial to adjust the angle of the ball for return—much like the Pong games, created by Nolan Bushnell, that would appear fourteen years later.

By the early 1970s, computer games began cropping up at universities, being played in the off-hours. Professors at Dartmouth became frustrated with the students gaming because of the time-share rules in using the machines. They responded by creating games with education content. Physics professor Art Luehrmann created the game Potshot to teach the principles of projectile motion.

From the 1970s, computer gaming consoles became regular fixtures in family rooms across America. Atari, ColecoVision, and Intellevision begat PC games, Nintendo, Sega, Sony Playstation, Xbox, and other consoles. We now also find computer games on handheld computers, cell phones, and the Internet (see MUDs). Computer games are becoming more interactive. Using the Internet, players can join others in many different forms of games, graphical and text-based. The new gaming consoles also allow gaming over the Internet, provided the players have the same hardware and software. Games are so popular that Hollywood has had huge success with game-based movies such as *Tomb Raider.* In fact, in 2001 the game industry outstripped Hollywood's box-office revenues, with consumers purchasing $9.4 billion worth of gaming hardware and software. Several home video game consoles also offer CD and DVD playback.

BIBLIOGRAPHY

Ahl, D.H. (1983). "Editorial." *Video and Arcade Games* 1(1). Available at <http://cvmm.vg-network.com/vag1.htm>.

Croal, N. (2002). "Now, Video Verite." *Newsweek* 139(22) (June 3), p. 43.

Goldberg, M. (n.d.). "The History of Computer Gaming." Available at <http://www.classicgaming.com/features/articles/computergaminghistory/>.

Geek Speak

Often referred to as "techno-babble" or "techno-speak," *geek speak* (jargon) is a growing lexicon of slang terms and phrases used by technologists and hobbyists alike, ranging from software to hardware to Star Trek and beyond. An example: "We'll need to kludge around a bit to fix that bug in the system." Translation: "We're going to avoid some computer problems by working around them."

As with any community, the sequential nature of language facilitates a description of our world. Lawyers use words such as "whereupon" and "heretofore" both out of tradition and, in a way, to remain a specialized community. Sylvia Adamson (1992), author of a review of *The Oxford Companion to the English Language* titled "The Language of Language," continues: "The specialization of discourses is one of the tragedies of our time: increasingly, each branch of study entrenches itself behind a technical terminology that separates, or alienates, the interested amateur from the specialist and creates tortuous rites of passage" (p. 9). Although these discourses are necessary to allow for the precise identification of certain concepts, they are often used to provide a more technical-sounding equivalent of a plain-English idea. Jargon obscures simple ideas in gratuitously complex phraseology. As journalist William Zinsser (1976) writes, "Every profession has its growing arsenal of jargon to fire at the layman and hurl him back from its walls" (p. 15). However, as new members join the community, this new language is learned.

Here are a few examples of geek speak from *The Urban Geekosphere* (Naudus, n.d.):

> alpha geek (n) ["alpha male"]: The most technically accomplished or skillful person in some implied context. "Ask Larry, he's the alpha geek here."
> glomp (v): To aggressively hug someone about the neck, usually from a running start resulting in the perpetuator smacking up against the victim.

multitasking (n) /1: The ability of a computer to run several programs simultaneously. /2: When a person does several things at the same time.

PEBKAC (n) ["Problem Exists Between Keyboard And Chair"]: Technical support acronym indicating the dilemma originates from the customer's own base stupidity. This is true in the case of most technical support calls.

xerophilia (n) ["xerox"]: The love of copying and the ability of everything to be copied.

BIBLIOGRAPHY

Adamson, S. (1992). "The Language of Language." *The New York Times Literary Supplement* (December 11), p. 9.

Blodgett, M. (2002). "How to Translate Geek Speak." *CIO Magazine* (January 1).

Candido, A.M. (1999). "Fabricating and Prefabricating Language: Troubling Trends in Libraries." *Journal of Academic Librarianship* 25(6) (November).

Naudus, K. (n.d.). *The Urban Geekosphere.* Available at <http://www.urbangeek.net>.

Sandberg, J. (1998). "The Perils of Geek Speak." *Newsweek* 132(25) (December 21), p. 77.

Zinsser, W. (1976). *On Writing Well.* New York: Harper and Row, p. 15.

Global Positioning Systems

One of the greatest fears that can strike the hearts of parents is that of losing a child. Being lost in the wilderness or off a roadside as the result of misdirection or an accident is another scary scenario. Not being able to keep up with parolees or probationers is a problem for law enforcement officers. What do these dilemmas have in common? GPS, or Global Positioning Systems, promise to solve them all.

Owned and operated by the U.S. Department of Defense, the Global Positioning System consists of twenty-four carefully spaced and arranged satellites that make it possible to pinpoint geographic locations using special receivers. Accuracy as precise as within one meter can be achieved with specialized military equipment, or within 10 to 100 meters with less sophisticated mechanisms. Anybody can buy a GPS receiver for less than $200 at stores such as Wal-Mart and Academy. GPS receivers are increasingly popular with hunters, boaters, and other sports enthusiasts. Not only can a GPS device tell the user where he or she is, it can also provide directions. By hooking up a GPS receiver with a computer that has downloaded detailed maps, a traveler can map out a route, including details such as restaurants and hotels. Hunting and fishing guides with landmarks, fishing holes, and other data are available for outdoor enthusiasts.

GPS devices are also appearing in cars, helping drivers locate destinations and plan alternate routes when weather or traffic interruptions occur, and assisting the unwary who lose their way. In some school districts, buses are equipped with GPS to allow tracking at all times.

People also are being tracked with GPS. Security bracelets or ankle guards are used to track the movement of parolees. Similar devices are available for parents, such as a lockable bracelet designed for use with children up to twelve years in age. They are also being touted as useful for elderly people with Alzheimer's or other disorders who are at risk of straying and then being unable to get their bearings on their own. GPS chips can be packaged in devices about the size of pagers and attached to clothing. People are even considering GPS for pets that are prone to wander. If a wanderer, be it oldster, child, or pooch, goes beyond preset parameters, an alarm can be sent to the caretaker's cell phone or pager. Future developments are expected to include making the chips so small that they can be sewn into clothing. Thus in coming days, people can always figure out where they are, but of course everyone else may know as well.

BIBLIOGRAPHY

Schwartz, E. (2002). "Wireless Peace of Mind." *InfoWorld* 24 (February 25), p. 28.
"Something to Watch Over You." *The Economist* 374 (August 17), pp. 61-64.
Taylor, R. (2002). "New Directions." *Popular Mechanics* 170 (June), pp. 98-102.

Globalization

"The new electronic interdependence recreates the world in the image of a global village" (McLuhan, 1962). McLuhan continues that electronic "discoveries" have recreated a sense that all of humanity resides in a single theoretical living space where compartmentalizing individual human potential no longer makes sense, though we are all unwilling to give up our individual identities. In a way, McLuhan holds, new technology brings us back to a tribal society.

Globalization, through technology, blurs all geographic, ideological, cultural, and societal boundaries. Television, copper wire, fiber optics, satellite and cellular telecommunications, and the Internet allow access to anyone, anytime, anywhere. Our world is shrinking. It is interesting to follow the progression in thinking of our world: the world is flat, the world is round, the world is global.

Economists follow that globalization is a powerful trend, driven by a combination of technological developments, profit-seeking businesses, and public policy. Globalization, simply, is an expansion of possible commercial activities. Acts of buying, selling, and producing, previously hindered by geographic, technological, or legal borders, have now become practical. Determining and organizing the possibilities opened up by technology for globalization requires great effort, flexibility, and change; however, globalization offers a marvelous array of new opportunities. But is this true for everyone?

According to the *World Telecommunication Development Report: Reinventing Telecoms* (ITU, 2002), the quality of and access to the Internet is increasingly worsening; and while the general use of telephone services are growing, this growth comes from a very low base. United Nations Secretary General Kofi Annan reported that the Internet is used by 5 percent of the world's population. Some 85 percent of all users and 90 percent of hosts are in developed countries. Additional research by Ernest J. Wilson III, University of Maryland, shows that in 2000, 98 percent of Latin Americans, 99.5 percent of Africans, and 98 percent of Asians did not have access to the Internet.

So technology does increase access to information and individuals, but perhaps only to those whom already had this access. There seems to be no question in some circles, though, that with newer, cheaper technologies (e.g., mobile devices), access will expand and boundaries will become blurred even further. We'll have to wait to see.

BIBLIOGRAPHY

Conhaim, W.W. (2001). "The Global Digital Divide." *Information Today* 18(7) (July/August), pp. 1-3.

International Telecommunication Union (ITU) (2002). *World Telecommunication Development Report: Reinventing Telecoms.* United Nations: Geneva, Switzerland.

McLuhan, M. (1962). *The Gutenberg Galaxy: The Making of Typographic Man.* Toronto: University of Toronto Press.

McLuhan, M. (1996). *Essential McLuhan.* Edited by Eric McLuhan and Frank Zingrone. New York: Basic Books.

Taylor, T. (2002). "The Truth About Globalization." *The Public Interest* 147 (Spring), pp. 24-44.

Gopher

Gopher, named after the University of Minnesota's mascot, was a system for organizing and displaying files on Internet servers. It was the first Internet navigation tool and was a distributed document delivery system. It was an infoserver that could deliver text, graphics, audio, and multimedia to clients. This system was used, especially at universities, from 1992 through 1996. Organized text files could be brought from servers all over the world to one's computer. Gopher was a menu-based information searching tool that allowed users to access various types of databases, such as FTP archives and white pages databases. It was shortly replaced by the World Wide Web. Most databases have been converted to Web sites because they can be more easily accessed.

Two tools used for searching Gopher files were Veronica and Jughead. Veronica (very easy rodent-oriented netwide index of computerized archives) was an indexing program that visited Gopher sites, read all directory and file names, and then indexed them in one large index. In addition to native Gopher data, Veronica included references to many resources provided by other types of information servers, such as WWW servers, Usenet archives, and telnet-accessible information services. Veronica queries were keyword-in-title searches. A simple query could be quite powerful because a large number of information servers were included in the index. However, since most content has been put on the Web, Veronica has been used less and less. Jughead was similar to Veronica, but was not as powerful, and is now seldom-used. Jughead was used for searching the information on gopher sites for particular subjects. It could also be used to build a searchable menu of a particular Gopher hierarchy of menus.

There are still hundreds of Gopher sites around the world. To see a list of some of them, assuming your site has a Gopher "client" installed, you can reach them by typing "gopher _____" (the site name).

BIBLIOGRAPHY

Carvin, A. (n.d.). "WWW History: The Birth of On-Line Multimedia." Available from <http://www.edwebproject.org/web.future.html>.

Gaffin, A. and Heitkotter, J. (1994). *Big Dummy's Guide to the Internet.* Available from <http://www.nectec.or.th/net-guide/bigdummy/bdg_181.html#SEC184>.

"Gopher." (2002). Available from <http://www.computeruser.com/resources/dictionary/definition.html?lookup=2408>.

Karger, B. (2002). "The Gopher://Manifesto." Available from <http://www.scn.org/~bkarger/gopher-manifesto>.

Graphical User Interface

Most of us use a graphical user interface or GUI (pronounced "gooey") every day. A computer's operating system, such as MS Windows is, probably, the most popular example. The use of a GUI-based operating system allows for the simple point-and-click or point-and-double-click thus avoiding typing numerous commands and codes just to run a program. A GUI also includes what the user sees on the screen: windows, icons, and other interactive objects.

The first GUI appeared in 1974 for the Alto workstation. This was not like the GUIs of today, but rather included graphically driven programs featuring bit mapping such as the drawing program, Markup, the painting program, Superpaint, and Bravo, a text editor.

In 1981, Xerox's Palo Alto Research Center (PARC) was using its WIMP (Windows, Icons, Menus, and Pointers) GUI for the Xerox Star. It is widely rumored that this is the GUI that Steve Jobs "borrowed" for the Apple Macintosh computer. However, a deal was made between Xerox and Apple that allowed Jobs and staff to visit PARC and take notes while Xerox obtained a block of Apple stock.

By the end of that year, Jobs gave a presentation of the new Macintosh and its GUI operating system and authorized Microsoft to develop applications for the new computer. During the years 1981 to 1984, Microsoft programmers became familiar with the new GUI, and two months before the Macintosh was introduced to the world in 1984, Microsoft announced that it, too, would be offering its own GUI for PCs. It is interesting that also during this time, IBM was not interested in Microsoft's GUI-based operating system. Big Blue had already been using Microsoft's MS-DOS, but thought that the GUI interface for PCs was a fad. Microsoft Windows 1.0 was released in November 1985.

Many other types of GUIs are utilized in technology. Operating systems, such as Linux and X-Windows for computers, Windows CE, Symbian, and Palm OS for PDAs and cell phones, as well as simple GUIs that are used in home audio/video remote controls, washer/

dryers, refrigerators, vending machines; the list goes on. As we strive for simpler technology, point-and-click or even touch will be utilized on more devices—current and emergent—using the international language of pictures and images, much like signs and labels.

BIBLIOGRAPHY

Tuck, M. (n.d.). "The Real History of the GUI." Available at <http://www.Webmasterbase.com/article/511/99>.

History of Computer Hardware

People tend to think of the computer as a development of the twentieth century, but predecessors can be traced far back into history. As early as 450 B.C. the abacus was used for computations, and other early devices for keeping up with numbers include the Aztec calendar. The first mechanical calculator, used for addition, subtraction, multiplication, and division, was developed by a German mathematician named Wilhelm Schikard in the early seventeenth century. Soon after, in 1642, Frenchman Blaise Pascal built an adding and subtracting machine. His accomplishment was honored in the naming of Pascal, a modern computer language.

The use of machines to complete an operation other than computation came with Jacquard's loom. French inventor Joseph-Marie Jacquard wanted a device that would automatically execute weaving operations for rugs. In 1800 he came up with the idea of using punched paper cards to communicate the patterns he wanted the looms to weave. The use of punched cards was to play an important part in future devices as well. Charles Babbage, a British mathematician who moved closer to concepts shared with today's computers, adopted the card system. The reclusive Babbage built two machines, completed in 1834, called the Difference Engine and the Analytical Engine. In the Difference Engine resided numbers to be operated upon, which he called the "store." The Analytical Engine was the "mill," which he designed to perform the operations. This was done by the use of two sets of punched cards: one prescribed operations and the other provided the variables with which to work. Babbage was assisted by Ada Byron, Lady Lovelace, who was the daughter of the famous poet, Lord Byron. She wrote the directions for the Analytical Engine, which came to be called "programs." Ada is remembered as the first computer programmer, and a U.S. Department of Defense computer programming language was named in her honor. The importance of the Babbage computer went virtually unrecognized at the time, and Babbage died without knowing how influential his work would be.

This *Scientific American* cover depicts use of the latest high-tech development of the time, the Electrical Enumerator Machine. It was used in the U.S. Census of 1890, which completed in one month the same processes that had taken ten years to complete with the previous 1880 census. (*Source:* "The New Census of the United States—The Electrical Enumerator Machine." *Scientific American* [August 20, 1890], from Washington, DC: Library of Congress Prints and Photographs Collection.)

Charles Babbage, whose Difference Engine and Analytical Engine laid the groundwork for the development of modern computers. (*Source:* "The Late Mr. Babbage," *The Illustrated London News* [November 4, 1871]. From Washington, DC: Library of Congress Prints and Photographs Collection.)

Today Charles Babbage is remembered as the father of modern computing.

The complexities of a developing country in an increasingly industrial age drove the need to realize the potential of computing machines. The U.S. Census of 1880 took ten years to complete due to the lack of efficient means to handle the data, so that by the time it was completed, a new census was due. This fiasco inspired two census bureau employees, Herman Hollerith and John Billings, to devise a machine that used punched cards for representing and sorting data. The resulting system was so successful that data from the next census were processed in only a month. Hollerith went on to found the Tabulating Machine Company in an effort to market the invention. Punched cards came to be called Hollerith cards and were used in an ever-growing number of situations, continuing into the 1960s and 1970s. As for the Tabulating Machine Company, a young employee named

Ada, Lady Lovelace, was the daughter of the poet Lord Byron and has been called the first computer programmer. She wrote the directions for Babbage's Analytical Engine and thus proved that from the earliest history, women had a vital role in the development of computer technology. (*Source: Ada, Lady Lovelace.* Washington, DC: Library of Congress Prints and Photographs Collection.)

Thomas J. Watson gained control in 1924 and changed the name to the International Business Machine Company. IBM was born.

Refinements continued through the 1930s and 1940s, including the construction of a specialized computer for solving linear equations using vacuum tubes for data storage. Military applications of the newly emerging technology grew out of the need to compute ballistics during World War II. The resulting device was called the Electronic Numerical Integrator and Computer, or ENIAC. This computer, huge and slow by today's standards, was designed, or "hardwired," to calculate trajectories of missiles. The time difference for computations as compared to previous methods was awesome—twenty hours' work could be done in just thirty seconds with ENIAC.

The success of ENIAC resulted in increased interest and demand for computational devices. However, vacuum tubes were problematic due to their high failure rates and the space they required. Refinements ensued over the next few years, including Jon von Neumann's conceptualizing of a machine capable of completing more than one specific and limited task. His new device was called EDVAC (electronic discrete variable automatic computer), and was produced around 1950.

During the next twenty years, transistors brought new options for making computers smaller and faster. IBM entered the commercial market in 1948 and was a dominant force in the coming decades. Mainframe computers became increasingly powerful and important in more diverse settings.

The next big change for computers was the advent of smaller machines, minicomputers in the 1970s and microcomputers in the 1980s. Increasing speed and decreasing size are ongoing trends into the 2000s as devices continue to get smaller, faster, more versatile, and more important to daily work and life.

BIBLIOGRAPHY

Edgar, S. (2002). *Morality and Machines: Perspectives on Computer Ethics.* Boston, MA: Jones and Bartlett.

Murdoch, J. (1998). *Internet Timeline.* Available from <http://www.mcc.murdoch. edu.au/ReadingRoom/VID/jfk/timeline.htm>.

Park, K. (2002). "Computer Milestones." *World Almanac and Book of Facts 2002.* New York: World Almanac Publications.

Schoenherr, S. (1999). "Jacquard's Punched Card." *Smithsonian National Museum of American History Picture List.* Available from <http://history.acusd.edu/gen/ recording/jacquard1.html>.

Hoax Sites

Internet hoax sites are published to display Webmasters' creative abilities, to provide sites for exercise in Web site evaluation, and for the sheer fun of it. Such sites present erroneous and often outlandish information as fact. Disclaimers that explain that such sites are not "real" are usually present but inconspicuous. Probably the most famous and extensive site is the one touting the wonders of Mankato, Minnesota. According to the homepage, hot springs in the area allow the town to enjoy balmy weather even during Minnesota's notoriously harsh winters. Travelers can, according to the pages, enjoy an underwater world park featuring a tube beneath the Minnesota River, a pyramid that bears a striking resemblance to the Egyptian pyramids, a mountain ski area, and numerous other incredible attractions, backed up by staged photos and fictitious references. This site was developed by a University of Minnesota professor for the purpose of sharpening student skills and providing an evaluation site for others. An element of veracity is lent to the site by the fact that there really is a town of Mankato. One would think that such unlikely claims would be obvious tips that the site was bogus, but amazingly it has managed to fool many unwary Internet surfers, some of whom actually made trips to Mankato to enjoy the diversions. The Mankato Chamber of Commerce even objected and asked the professor and his students to take down the site because it was misleading and detracted from Mankato's true charms. This delighted the site's developers, who are continually revising and gleefully updating the site, adding even more false claims. A companion site named *New Hartford, Minnesota,* extols the virtues of a mythical wonderland, a completely made-up town supposedly located in south-central Minnesota, and is linked to the Mankato site.

Hoax sites deal with many topics other than phony travel tips. Another perennial favorite is "Feline Reactions to Bearded Men," supposedly exploring how cats react to hirsute human males. The site follows through all the steps of the scientific process, making it an excellent choice for use with science students. A perusal of the "experts" listed in the site's bibliography should suffice in making it clear that the presentation is tongue in cheek.

Many hoax sites have short lives. Because they are not bona fide presentations supported by actual locations, businesses, or other concerns, they tend to disappear and sometimes reappear at the whims of their creators. Finding them is easy, though, by conducting an Internet search using the words "Internet hoax sites." Such sites are fun to visit and are also excellent tools in demonstrating the fact that not everything one encounters in exploring the World Wide Web is true.

BIBLIOGRAPHY

Farnsworth, R.B. (2003). *Mankato, Minnesota Home Page.* Available from <http://www.lme.mankato.msus.edu/mankato/mankato.html>.

Goff, L. (1998). "Hoax on You." *Computerworld* (May 25), p. 71.

Humphries, L. (2000). "Teaching Users to Evaluate Internet Sites: Sources ON Sources." *Searcher* 8 (May), pp. 68-70.

Johnson, S. (2002). *New Hartford, Minnesota.* Available from <http://www.lme.mnsu.edu/newhartford/newhtfd.html>.

HTML

HTML stands for hypertext markup language. It is the code used to program Web pages. Hypertext works like a cross-reference in a book. By following a link, the user reaches another gateway to similar or dissimilar information. This information then offers links to other gateways where one may jump again. Hypertext pages typically feature multiple links, offering multiple gateways to multiple paths of information. This is how the World Wide Web works.

HTML is a nonproprietary format that can be created and processed by a wide range of tools, from a simple plain text editor, such as Windows Notepad or WYSIWYG (pronounced "wizzy wig"), or "what you see is what you get" Web page design tools, such as Macromedia Dreamweaver. HTML is standardized by the W3C, the World Wide Web Consortium, which develops interoperable technologies, guidelines, software, and tools for the Web. The following is a short example of HTML code:

```
<html>
  <head>
    <title>Hello World!</title>
  </head>
  <body>
    <p>Hello to all who see this page!</p>
  </body>
</html>
```

This code places the words "Hello World!" along the top title bar on a Web browser, and the words "Hello to all who see this page!" within the page of the browser. The <html> tag tells the browser that a Web page is about to begin. The <head> tag tells the browser how to display the page, e.g., fonts, colors, and/or title, as shown here. <body> tells the browser to expect and how to handle the main page. <p> marks the beginning of a paragraph. Any tag with a slash, e.g.,

</html>, tells the browser it is at the end of the section or end of the page.

Each new version of HTML allows for better design and greater interactivity, including tables, multimedia, graphics, fonts, etc. HTML is a design standard and is utilized on many types of devices beyond computers: cell phones, handheld computers, CDs, and DVDs.

BIBLIOGRAPHY

Burke, J. (1999). *The Knowledge Web: From Electronic Agents to Stonehenge and Back—and Other Journeys Through Knowledge.* New York: Simon and Schuster.

W3C HTML Home Page (n.d.). <http://www.w3c.org/MarkUp/>.

Hyperfiction

Hyperfiction, also called interactive fiction, hypertext fiction, or nonlinear fiction, is an evolving genre. It consists of text presented in computer format, usually via the Internet, that is written in hypertext and has the feature of allowing the reader to pursue the path of his or her choice by following the hyperlinks embedded in the text. The reader can follow multiple paths through the same text with variable developments and possible outcomes. Enhancements such as maps, charts, illustrations, etc., are included as well, and are made accessible through hyperlinks. Thus, according to proponents, the reader becomes an active participant in the evolution of the story or of his or her experience in appreciating the presentation. The reader finds the experience enhanced by the combination of choice in the direction the story takes and the resulting unexpected twists and turns the narrative thereby offers. The term "hypertext" was coined in the 1970s by Theodor Nelson, who first used it to describe nonlinear writing made possible for composing and reading in computer format. Early writers include Michel Joyce, Professor of English at Vassar College, who began writing in this fashion in the early 1990s. Joyce created a software application, called Storyspace, which he continues to use for his own writing and which has been used by a number of writers, instructors, and students. Popularity of this new format, which began in America, has extended to Europe and Japan. Hyperfiction works are most commonly accessible via the Internet, but can also be presented on CD-ROM or disks. A number of university professors and students are turning to hyperfiction as a creative genre to explore and develop. Hyperfiction requires a different sort of writer and reader, with the writer willing and able to incorporate various directions and options in his or her work, and the reader willing to join in the experience by choosing the direction of it rather than accepting the more traditional and passive role of reading a linear piece.

Collaborative hyperfiction, a spin-off from hypertext narratives, can trace its lineage back to primitive campfire storytelling sessions.

In these creations, a story is posted to the Internet with provision for the readers to contribute to it and add their own developments, illustrations, etc. Thus the work becomes an ever-changing and growing production with an unlimited number of contributors.

The genre of hyperfiction is at present in its evolutionary stages. The importance of the genre is difficult to gauge, but has been described by Mihajlovic (1998) in these terms: "Literature can be divided into two currents, the first being the noninteractive works and the second, the interactive works, and the future of fiction lies in this distinction" (p. 221).

BIBLIOGRAPHY

Mihajlovic, J. (1998). "Milorad Pavic and Hyperfiction." *Review of Contemporary Fiction* 18 (Summer), pp. 214-221.

Morgan, W. and Andrews, R. (1998). "City of Text? Metaphors for Hypertext in Literary Education." *Changing English: Studies in Reading and Culture* 18 (Summer), pp. 214+.

Vander Veer, E. (2001). "E-genres." *Writer* 114 (April), pp. 16+.

Hypertext

Prior to the 1970s computer text files were primarily plain text files containing straight presentations of characters without specialized formatting or interactive links. All that changed with the advent of hypertext, said by many to be the inspiration of the Internet as it exists today. Theodor Nelson coined the term "hypertext" in the 1960s to describe his conceptualization of a new form of electronic text that would be nonsequential rather than linear. Such text would allow readers to branch off in an endless array of directions, according to their interests and needs. He began working on a program, dubbed Xanadu, to achieve this purpose.

From this grew the system of linking one document to another, allowing the vast Web of interconnecting information sources that is the Internet. Hypertext development has not been without growing pains. Linking documents leads to questions of copyright, misappropriation, and other misuses of people's creations displayed on the Internet. A pertinent, but yet-to-be-resolved question is exactly when and under what circumstances a Webmaster is legally constrained to obtain permission before linking his or her page to another. If regulations are overly restrictive, the result may be a loss of the interactivity and flexibility that makes the Internet appealing.

Meanwhile, Nelson has described himself as less than satisfied with the ways in which hypertext has evolved. He sees it as falling short of the fluidity he imagined originally, and has stated that it is governed by engineers, less spontaneous and adaptable than it might be otherwise. Because hypertext differs dramatically from linear text, it is a realm that is emerging and developing as the Internet continues to grow.

BIBLIOGRAPHY

Edwards, O. (1997). "Ted Nelson." *Forbes* 160 (August 25), pp. 134-136.

aries to the extent that a user can, using electronic technology, be in any country (and, interestingly, any time zone) just by changing the URL address in a browser. The advent of the Internet has fostered an enormous increase in the population with direct access to huge amounts of information; local and global. As the need for international policy for use and information sharing increases, technology continues to push the way governments rethink agency roles; changing roles, changing policy, changing procedure, changing culture.

BIBLIOGRAPHY

Botstein, L. (2001). "High-Tech 'Brave New World' Braggadocio." *The Education Digest* 66(9) (May), pp. 11-16.
Matthews, J.T. (2000). "The Information Revolution." *Foreign Policy* 119 (Summer), pp. 63-65.

Instant Messaging

Instant messaging and e-mail are closely related with one major difference. Instant messaging allows for continued exchange rather than the back-and-forth exchange made possible by e-mail. The ability to see whether another user is connected to the Internet and exchange messages has found a wide audience. Instant messaging requires that both parties be online at the same time. The recipient must also be willing to accept messages, since most instant messaging software allows users to reject messages. America Online (AOL) is often credited as the first provider to popularize instant messaging. When an instant message is sent, the recipient will hear a sound indicating that he or she has a message. Instantaneous receiving and sending instant messages is almost like having a real conversation with another person. It is also possible to carry on a conversation with more than one person; just be careful that you are sending the right message to the right recipient.

Instant messaging was created in 1996 by four Israeli programmers, Yair Goldfinger, Arik Vardi, Sefi Vigiser, and Amnon Amir, who felt people were connected via the Internet, but not interconnected. Their program, ICQ ("I seek you"), registered more than 850,000 users within its first six months of release. It was sold to AOL in 1998.

At first, instant messaging was considered more of a toy. It has since become a vital and strategic tool for many companies, which see the value of maintaining instant communication in the workplace.

BIBLIOGRAPHY

Gittlen, S. (2003). "Instant Messaging Getting its Due?" Available from <http://www.nwfusion.com/ns/getsmart/ARCHIVES/041603.html>.

Karandish, D. (2003). "The Future of Instant Messaging." Available from <http://www.encore-designs.com/aimtalk/aol-instant-messenger-future.html>.

Whatis.com (n.d.). "Instant Messaging." *Whatis?com's Encyclopedia of Technology Terms.* Indianapolis, IN: Que, p. 348.

Internet Acronyms

According to Webster's, an *acronym* is a word formed from the initial letter or letters of each of the successive parts or major parts of a compound term. Acronyms may be formed by using existing words, in which phrase name is designed to fit the acronym. An example of this is BASIC, which stands for Beginner's All-Purpose Symbolic Instruction Code. Sometimes initialism is used, in which a new word is formed using the initial letters. An example is ASAP, which stands for "as soon as possible."

Users often use abbreviations, initialism, or acronyms that are unique to the Internet, but many words may be familiar in other areas as well. True Internet acronyms are probably not as familiar to most as those used in chat rooms and instant messages.

Some examples of Internet acronyms include the following:

- ADP: automatic data processing
- HTML: hypertext markup language
- HTTP: hypertext transfer protocol
- LAN: local area network
- SAP: service access point or service advertising protocol
- SNAP: subnetwork access protocol
- TRIP: token ring interface processor
- VAD: voice activity detection

However, the following list of terms used in chat rooms, instant messages, or e-mails will be more familiar.

- B4: before
- BFN: bye for now
- BTW: by the way
- GAL: get a life
- IDK: I don't know
- IOW: in other words

- KIT: keep in touch
- OIC: oh, I see
- YOYO: you're on your own

Other abbreviations do not fit into any of these categories. These include the use of characters to express emotions or feelings (see "Emoticons," p. 72). The symbol used most commonly is the sideways smiley face formed by the characters of a semicolon and right parenthesis mark :). Emoticons will be used more often as acronyms or abbreviations are invented to save time when communicating.

BIBLIOGRAPHY

Cisco Systems, Inc. (2001). "Internetworking Terms and Acronyms." *Dictionary of Internetworking Terms and Acronyms.* Available from <http://www.cisco.com/univercd/cc/td/doc/cisintwk/ita/index.htm>.

Merriam Webster Online (n.d.). "Acronym." Available from <http://www.m-w.com/>.

Netlingo.com (n.d.). "Acronyms and Shorthand." Available from <http://www.netlingo.com/emailsh.cfm>.

Whatis.com (n.d.). "Acronym." Available from <http://whatis.techtarget.com/definition/0,,sid9_ gci211518,00.html>.

Internet Advertising

Internet advertising can be described as boon or bane, depending on one's viewpoint. Because many Web sites and free services exist only due to funds garnered from advertising, it follows that without these ads the Net would lose many entertaining and informational sites. In addition, Web resources would have to resort to subscription charges and other fees in order to exist. The idea of free access is one of the most treasured attributes of the Internet, so advertising is likely here to stay.

In the beginning, banners at the tops of pages were the most common Internet ads. Banners have evolved from the original static displays to flashing, moving presentations with interactive features. All the same, people have a way of disregarding banners; studies show them to generate low interest and response from Web surfers. As a result, enterprising advertisers have come up with an array of additional ploys to attract and often demand attention. Pop-ups leap into view upon access to a site, irritating many Internet users as well as gaining attention. Pop-unders were soon to follow, bringing up the ad unbeknownst to the user until he or she shut down all pages to log off. Mouse-overs cause a display to appear when the user's mouse rolls over a certain point on a site, only to disappear when it moves away.

Many advertisers compete for attention by offering free giveaways. As with responding to other forms of contests and giveaways such as mailers and mall drawings, the person who bites on the free giveaway hook also gives away personal information. To advertisers, this data is like money in the bank and results in the entrant getting, as one might easily guess, more advertising. Early efforts at information gathering in this manner were amazingly successful, proving again P. T. Barnum's maxim about a sucker born every minute. Consequently, the future will certainly hold plenty of flashy Internet ads with enticing offers in the form of contests and giveaways.

Unfortunately, the downside to Internet advertising goes beyond irritating and uninvited displays. Advertisements for pornography have appeared in increasing numbers, even showing up on reliable sites such as Yahoo. Some ads spawn others, opening multiple browser windows, which then must be closed one by one, a practice bordering on harassment. In an effort to get some relief from the advertising glut, users are turning to ad-blocking software. A *blocking application* is software that resides between an Internet connection and a browser. When one clicks on a link, the program checks the HTML code and screens out the ads, allowing only the desired page to be displayed. Further constraints may come from an organization called the Interactive Advertising Bureau, a private agency that has voiced concerns about unethical advertising practices. Finally, there is hope that advertisers will figure out that irritating and offending their potential customers hardly promotes goodwill.

Another way the Internet can deliver advertising is through e-mail. Advertisers who get information through giveaway and contest promotions are sure to follow up with e-mail, just as responding to contests offline results in phone calls and junk mail. One reason these practices continue is that they work. In 2000 a popular musical group, *NSYNC, sent out a mass e-mail to fans, with a video message containing greetings from band members and a snippet from their newest song. The resulting sales were phenomenal, causing this type of promotion to gain immediate attention from other advertisers. E-mail messages often contain invisible HTML tools that allow the sender to know how often and by whom messages are opened. Messages that invite recipients to reply and request no future contact are really just confirming the address of the person responding, so that additional ads can be sent. Filters and specialized blocking software can eliminate some unwanted messages, but inventive marketers often find ways to circumvent such attempts.

As long as Internet sites and services are funded largely by advertisements, marketers will find as many ways as possible to reach the public. Users will continue to benefit from free access to a wealth of resources while making good use of their delete buttons in e-mail and closing unwanted browser sites.

BIBLIOGRAPHY

Gann, R. (2001). "Ad-Blocking Software Pulling the Plugs." *Internet Magazine* (November), pp. 106-115.

McDermott, I. (1998). "Free Stuff on the Web." *Searcher* (October), p. 36.

Internet Providers

Internet providers are of two types. One is the Internet service provider (ISP), which provides the backup for the Internet access provider. The other is the Internet access provider (IAP), which is the company that provides individuals or companies access to the Internet. The Internet service provider has the equipment and telecommunication systems for the geographic area being served. The ISP provides the user with a software package and also charges a monthly fee, which varies among the many providers available. The user will then choose a username, a password, and an access phone number. Equipped with a modem, the user can then log on to the Internet and browse the World Wide Web and send or receive e-mail.

There are literally hundreds of ISPs across the country. Some of these provide service to a very small area only, whereas others, such as AOL, provide online service to most of the country. These larger ISPs interconnect with one another through switching centers.

The Directory of Internet Service Providers is a list of service providers that can be accessed online. The list can be accessed by area code, country code, the United States, and Canada. The list attempts to give only reliable providers and recommends that one verifies the provider's reputation.

BIBLIOGRAPHY

Howe, W. (2001). "A Brief History of the Internet." Available from <http://www.walthowe.com/ navnet/history.html>.

"Internet Access Provider." Available from <http://searchWebServices.techtarget.com/sDefinition/0,,sid26_gci214092,00.html>.

Jupitermedia Corporation (2003). *The Directory of Internet Service Providers.* Available from <http://thelist.internet.com>.

"Network Service Provider." Available from <http://searchWebServices.techtarget.com/sDefinition/0,,sid26_gci214028,00.html>.

Webopedia.com (n.d.). "ISP." Available from <http://www.Webopedia.com/TERM/I/ISP.html>.

Internet Radio

Internet radio, sometimes called *Web radio,* is "radio without airwaves, which is to say it's technically not radio" (Cartensen, 2000, p. 1). Because it can be accessed via the World Wide Web, Internet radio is available to most online computer users. In 1993, Internet Talk Radio became the first radio station to broadcast on the Internet, and was followed by the first full-time, Internet-only station, Radio HK, in 1995.

In 1934, Congress passed the Communications Act, which established the Federal Communications Commission (FCC), and set the standard for regulating interstate and international communications by radio, television, wire, and, eventually, satellite and cable. For the most part, however, Internet radio stations are unregulated. With more Internet users availing themselves of this medium, many broadcasters are arguing for further governmental deregulation.

Thousands of stations all over the world now broadcast via the Internet. An online directory is available at <http://www.radiotower.com>. The directory lists more than 1,300 stations, which are searchable by name, country, and category. Once selected, a station's name and information, such as the type of music it plays, whether it is a news station, etc., is displayed. The stations are also rated by users. Depending on the speed of one's connection, some stations may take time to download. A similar directory is available at <http://www.web-radio.fm>.

Some advantages of Internet or Web radio are its diversity, clarity, and ability to reach a greater audience. Traditional radio stations can be heard only within the range of their broadcast signal, whereas Internet stations can be heard with clarity around the world.

According to author Chris Priestman (2002), Internet radio is defined more by the nature of its content than by its method of delivery. Starting an Internet radio station is relatively easy. "All you need besides the usual stereo equipment (microphone, CD player, mixer) is a PC, audio-encoding software (such as Shoutcast), and a fat connection to the Internet (such as a DSL line)—an initial investment of under $2,000" (Carstensen, 2000, p. 1). Unfortunately, it's not quite that simple. In 1998, Congress passed the Digital Millennium Copyright Act (DMCA), which established that Internet radio stations have to pay royalty fees based on the number of songs they play per listener. Following this act, many stations, often small, one-person operations, were forced to shut down rather than pay fees. In December 2002, President George W. Bush signed the Small Webcaster Settlement Act, which allows small Internet radio stations and the recording industry to negotiate lower royalty fees than those set in the DMCA. However, many station owners feel these acts will hinder the growth of Internet radio.

BIBLIOGRAPHY

Calypso, A. (2003). "Let the (Web) Music Play." *Black Enterprise* 33(11) (June), p. 57.

Carstensen, J. (2000). "Internet Radio." Available from <http://www.findarticles.com/cf_1/m)GER/2000_Spring/61426241/print.jhtml>.

Compaine, B. and Smith, E. (2001). "Internet Radio: A New Engine for Content Diversity?" Available from <http://itc.mit.edu/itel/docs/2001/compaine_smith_radio.pdf>.

Priestman, C. (2002). *Web Radio: Radio Production for Internet Streaming.* Oxford: Focal Press.

Wikipedia (2003). "History of Radio." Available from <http://www.wikipedia.org/wiki/Radio/History>.

IRC

Internet Relay Chat (IRC) is like CB radio for the Internet. Using a simple and free computer program, users can register for a chat account, and communicate with everyone else who is registered. The software program lets users know who is online and allows users to call one another. Users can also create buddy lists that are similar to an address book with speed dial. The user simply clicks on the username of the person he or she wishes to call and, if the other person is online, they are connected. Chat rooms are also available where many users can chat with everyone in the room. Moderators are often on hand to deal with users whose behavior becomes inappropriate.

While IRC is typically text-based, that is, users type what they would like to communicate to the other(s) and wait for a text reply, audio and some video capabilities are becoming more prevalent. In this, the software receives an Internet-based media broadcast and displays it within the chat software. Because of the potential for noise and confusion, this is usually limited to one broadcaster and several viewers or a one-on-one conversation. Audio and video are not yet used in chat rooms.

IRC gives users the ability to call anyone anywhere around the world, providing they are online. Some have used this as a way to avoid hefty telephone charges, especially internationally. Video chats, having been available to only wealthy corporations, are now in reach of the masses and are becoming increasingly powerful. Several software companies have released free or inexpensive Internet telephone software for just these capabilities. Because of technological limits such as echoing, poor sound quality, and bandwidth issues, most users use text-based chat only. As the technology improves, expect to see more multimedia-based chats.

BIBLIOGRAPHY

Baker, T. (2001). "Cut Through the Chatter." *Smart Computing* 12(6) (June), pp. 42-45.

Linux

Most computer users give little or no thought to the operating system they use. Windows, which in 2002 was on record for its presence on 90 percent of desktop computers, is so ubiquitous as to be assumed by many as the only way for computers to function. There is Mac OS, of course, but the trifling 5 percent of the market it garnered as of 2000 is of little consequence except to Mac enthusiasts. However, another option exists, one whose devotees are almost evangelical. Linux is hailed by many as the best operating system around.

People who extol the virtue of Linux praise open-source code—software that is not strictly controlled and, to a degree, can be controlled by the user. Another big plus Linux enthusiasts like to push is the fact that it is free. Early adopters of Linux claim that it is nearly crash proof, compared to Windows, which can frequently freeze or crash. Linux users tend to be technology devotees rather than mainstream users who simply want the convenience of Windows and the productivity programs it offers. Linux promoters hope to break into the mainstream with their own productivity and software alternatives, such as StarOffice, designed to compete with Microsoft Office.

Downsides for Linux users include the fact that most software is designed for Windows operating systems or possibly for Macintosh. Furthermore, some doubt whether Linux will remain free. Whether the promise of wide acceptance of Linux, and whether it will result in more reliable, less crash-prone computing, remains to be seen.

BIBLIOGRAPHY

Manes, S. (2000). "Free at Last, Free Forever?" *PC World* 18 (April), p. 278.
Whatis.com (2002). "Linux." *Whatis?com's Encyclopedia of Technology Terms.* Indianapolis, IN: Que.

Luddite

Many times people will preface a statement that denigrates some aspect of technology with the disclaimer, "I'm no Luddite, but . . ." The term *Luddite* is used today to describe a person who fears or rejects technology. The origin of the word comes from nineteenth-century English history. One version of the term's origin says that "Ludds" or "Luddites" were followers of King Ludd, also known as Ned Ludd, who may or may not have been a real person. Supposedly, Ludd was a textile worker who smashed machines to protest their threat to the livelihoods of those working in the textile industry. They opposed the industrial revolution's increased use of textile and other machinery which resulted in a widespread loss of jobs for factory workers. They often operated under the cover of darkness, wearing masks and committing acts of vandalism. When the Luddites resorted to riots, their movement was crushed by the British army in bloody skirmishes.

The term came back into use in modern times and is applied to those who criticize or even question wholesale adoption of technology in any setting. Interestingly, the term has been adopted by a group calling themselves "Neo-Luddites." These are writers, philosophers, and social activists who voice skepticism about unquestioning adoption of a technology-driven society. They do not reject technology in toto, but question that it is always the best choice to meet every need or circumstance. Neo-Luddites remind people that at times simple tools are better than high-tech devices, that organic farming can be superior to chemically intensive methods, and that sometimes life is not enhanced by digital electronics. They claim to support moderation in the use of technology. Whether the term "Luddite" is an insult or a compliment depends to an extent on the opinion of the speaker, but its larger use remains derogatory.

BIBLIOGRAPHY

Whatis.com (2002). "Luddite." *Whatis?com's Encyclopedia of Technology Terms.* Indianapolis, IN: Que.

Winner, L. (1997). "Look Out For the Luddite Label." *Technology Review* 100 (November 21), p. 62.

Mac versus PC

For years there has been an ongoing debate between two zealously devoted groups of computer users: Macintosh devotees and Windows/PC fans. By the late 1990s the din of conflict subsided as Microsoft Windows became almost ubiquitous, claiming more than 90 percent of computer users. Mac aficionados, however, are extremely loyal, and the dispute between faithful users on both sides never completely dies.

Are there real differences between the two products? Mac is traditionally favored in graphic arts, whereas Windows has largely taken over the business world. Mac fans tout the user-friendly superiority of their favored product, but Windows has made great strides in usability. While Macs once dominated the educational market, the PC has replaced the Mac as the system of choice in most schools. Proponents of both systems will swear that theirs is faster. Macs are said to be less virus-prone. PC users will swear they have all the best games. In truth, many applications of all types are available for both platforms. Further, in recent years the Mac has provided cross-platform features that make going from one system to another generally a seamless transition.

In answer to the question of whether one system is superior to the other, the best response is that the potential buyer should become familiar with all options, know how he or she wants to use the computer, and ask which one best meets expectations. Beyond these admonitions, the choice is as it has always been—a personal one.

BIBLIOGRAPHY

Komando, K. (2000). "PC vs Mac: After Years of Debate, We Settle the Question Once and For All." *Popular Mechanics* 177 (July), 5-7.
Lenk, F. (1996). "Does Mac Still Matter?" *Chatelaine* 69 (June 1), 30.

Dr. Richard Crandall of Reed College poses with an early Apple computer. Crandall, a Reed classmate of Apple CEO Steve Jobs, was named a distinguished scientist at Apple. (*Source: Infonautics in the U.S.A.* 33 (1985). Washington, DC: The United States Information Agency.)

Media Streaming

Streaming has gained enormous popularity. It enables multimedia files to be broadcast over the Internet without requiring the viewer to download the file first, i.e., the media is played while it is being downloaded. Software plug-ins are run by Internet browsers to play media embedded in Web pages.

The average computer user can create multimedia content for streaming, often for little or no cost. PC and Macintosh users have access to free editing software with the purchase of a newer operating system. Windows offers Movie Maker and Apple offers iMovie. These software programs are simple, intuitive, and powerful. The user will also need a digital video (DV) camera. Nondigital video cameras will also work, but are slower and have a reduced quality. The computer should have a FireWire port. FireWire cards can be purchased for about $50. FireWire allows the DV camera to be plugged in directly to the computer, where the video signal is downloaded to the hard drive to be edited and compressed (see COMPRESSION) for an Internet stream.

Many media software companies are beginning to offer subscriptions to media streaming content. Real's RealOne player, for example, provides more than 100 "channels" to display news, sports, popular culture, music, and the weather for $9.95 per month. Other media players, such as Apple's QuickTime and Microsoft's Windows Media Player, offer similar capabilities—some media, of course, is free. As bandwidth increases, computer users will see more and better programming available for streaming. This will certainly compete with regular broadcast and cable television; or, networks will eventually see the possibilities and offer programming to TV sets over the Internet.

BIBLIOGRAPHY

Schlender, B. (2002). "The Real Deal." *Fortune* 145(5) (March 4), pp. 215-216, 220.

Wands, B. (2002). *Digital Creativity: Techniques for Digital Media and the Internet.* New York: John Wiley and Sons.

MIDI

In 1983 audiences at the first North American Music Manufacturers show in Los Angeles were amazed when two electronic instruments from different companies were connected together. Only one of the instruments was being played, but listeners were hearing both instruments. This demonstration introduced MIDI to the world.

MIDI, or Musical Instrument Digital Interface, use has grown to incorporate computers as musicians. By programming software packages, called "sequencers," in music notation, anyone can become a musician playing any instrument. MIDI instruments are typically piano-style keyboards that use wave table synthesis, hence, they are called synths. Wave table synthesis utilizes digital audio samples of individual or groups of instruments. For example, a single note on a violin is played in a studio, recorded digitally, and saved along with other recorded instruments on the synth's sound card. When a musician or computer instructs the synth to play the violin, the actual digital recording is played; for long notes, the tone is played in a loop. To play a different note than what was recorded, the synth speeds up or slows down the recording to achieve different tones. Because MIDI files are composed of code, much like an electronic text file, they are small and easily downloaded, e-mailed, and shared electronically.

The success of MIDI can be seen in several places on the Internet. Sites such as MIDIFarm.com offer MIDI file sharing, which is a boon to home recordists who may not have access to an entire band. Enthusiasts can direct an entire orchestra; the only limits are that of hardware.

For some time now, computer operating systems have had built-in MIDI players and decoders that allow practically any off-the-shelf sound card to offer MIDI instruments to the average user. There are even instances of software instruments that can be installed on a personal computer; Cubase VST is among the most popular. Because of the inexpensive nature and hardware compatibility of MIDI, many different types of electronics are being connected that might not oth-

This 1985 picture shows an early MIDI keyboard in use. (*Source: Infonautics in the U.S.A.* 5 (1985). Washington, DC: The United States Information Agency.)

erwise be. Home theaters, household lighting controls, and other systems use MIDI to communicate between household appliances. Home theater settings for multiple devices are controlled via electronic wired remote panels. MIDI hardware cables are also used for low-resistance, high-quality imaging and sound transfer between sources.

BIBLIOGRAPHY

Lipscomb, E. (1995). "How Much for Just the MIDI?" Available at <http://www. harmony-central.com/MIDI/Doc/intro.html>.

MP3s

MP3s are a recent version of the MPEG compression format, or Codec (see COMPRESSION). MPEG is a standard for compressing and coding audio/visual information for digital storage that was developed by the Moving Pictures Experts Group (MPEG). MPEG is a part of the International Standards Organization (ISO) and was established in 1988 to create efficient standards for audio/visual representation.

The MP3 standard is used primarily for audio. Using an MP3 program, users can "rip" tracks from their CDs to their hard drive. "Ripping a track" is computer jargon for copying a digital audio file from an audio CD to a computer hard drive. By using the software as a digital music library, users can create playlists—a list of songs from the library that can be of any genre, by any group, on any album; as long as the song is in the library. The MP3s and playlists can then be burned, or copied, to a blank audio CD or downloaded to an MP3 player device, such as the iPod or Rio. These are completely digital, portable audio playback devices, much like portable cassette players.

Some issues have arisen with the use of MP3s. Because they are digital files, MP3s can be sent via e-mail or shared over the Internet. Napster, for example, was a free file-sharing program that allowed literally millions of users to share music, without buying the CD or paying the artists and record companies.

Although Napster was eventually shut down by a federal judge, several other file-sharing services exist on the Internet, including Kazaa, LimeWire, and WinMX. A growing number of pay-per-play Web sites offer users access to audio downloads for a monthly subscription fee.

As file sharing became very popular with music, corporations began to see that this may also include videos, books, software, images, or anything else that can be digitized. Intellectual property and copyright laws and policies are designed to protect the interests of content creators and any royalties they may be afforded. Due to the ease of copying electronic works, several agencies, including the Recording Industry Association of America (RIAA), have taken legal steps against individuals for offering free copies of copyrighted materials on Internet computer servers. In response a new technology was developed jointly by IBM, Intel, Toshiba, and Matsushita Electric to give control back to copyright owners. The technology, Content Protection for Recordable Media, or CPRM, allows content producers to specify how many times a consumer can copy a file. When the consumer purchases and downloads a new album, the MP3 player would use a built-in CPRM rights-protection system, including a serial number already on the device's memory card or disk, to encrypt the file and create a unique "key." This key would let the music player know whether the file is stored on an authorized disk or memory chip. When the album is played, the player would check for the digital key; if the key fits, the file would be decrypted and the music will begin to play. The copy-protection system does not work unless it is deployed in the original files, in storage media, and in media players. This will foster a relationship between device makers and content creators to license the copy-protection technology and implement the system.

BIBLIOGRAPHY

Chiariglione, L. (2001). "MPEG: Achievements and Current Work." *International Organization for Standardization: Coding of Moving Pictures and Audio.* White paper, ISO/IEC JTC1/SC29/WG11.
Tristram, C. (2001). "The End of Free Music?" *Technology Review* 104(3) (April), pp. 29-30.

MUDs

Multi-user domains, or MUDs, are text-based virtual spaces and typically games. In MUDs, users are the authors, architects, and players; all collaboratively improvised. Building a MUD is a cross between writing fiction and computer programming. For example, designing a virtual wardrobe in a character's room involves writing text to describe the physicality and location of the wardrobe as well as writing the programming code to make the wardrobe exist within the physical dimensions of the virtual room. The characters users create for themselves are called personae. Most MUDs are role-playing games, such as Dungeons and Dragons. In fact, *MUD* originally referred to a "multi-user dungeon," a program in which the player in charge (usually the system administrator of the computer on which the MUD sits) is called the "Wizard" and has special permissions and commands available for maintaining and policing the MUD. The players are not only authors of the games, but of themselves as well. These players appear to be situated in an artificially constructed place that also hosts other players who are connected at the same time. These virtual spaces accept connections over a network, such as the Internet. These spaces hold rooms where players decide how they represent themselves; using usernames, rather than real names, describing themselves as female when they are actually male (and vice versa—gender swapping), changing physical appearance such as height, weight, hair, and eye color. Some players give extremely short descriptions, often cryptic. MUDers, on the whole, tend to keep to regular communities, much like a real-world pub. In this, different MUDs are different communities, following different social agreements on how the community behaves. MUDs provide an opportunity to try new identities for the construction and reconstruction of self. That is, you are who you pretend to be.

MUDs often host *bots* (small programs that run across a network and execute information gathering or processing tasks on behalf of the user). Players can interact with bots as with any other player; having conversations, playing together, and asking for help. An interesting twist in this is determining whether the bot is a real bot or simply another player pretending to be a bot. There are continual conversations on whether bots should be allowed in MUDs, and if so, should they be required to announce themselves as such.

When a player first enters a MUD, they find themselves at some landmark, such as a tree or a church. The player reads the description of their current locale as well as a description of their surroundings. The player then navigates through the area of the MUD, interacting with other players as they come upon them. The descriptions are also followed by a list of objects and characters. The player can earn and spend money, rise and fall in social status, and die.

MUDs can be extremely addictive to the player and can become an alternate reality. It is not unusual for a player to be logged on for six or more hours a day.

There are currently more than 300 active MUDs, averaging a total of 20,000 participants. Similar to MUDs are MMORPGs (Massively Multiplayer Online Roleplaying Games—the virtual descendents of MUDs). EverQuest, for example, has more than 500,000 subscribers with an average of 100,000 players online at any given time. MUDs and text-based chats have been likened to the CB radio phenomenon of the 1970s.

BIBLIOGRAPHY

Curtis, P. (1997). "Mudding: Social Phenomena in Text-Based Virtual Realities." In Kiesler, S. (ed.), *Culture of the Internet*. Mahwah, NJ: Lawrence Erlbaum Associates, pp. 121-142.

Turkle, S. (1995). *Life on the Screen: Identity in the Age of the Internet*. New York: Simon and Schuster.

Multimedia

Multimedia, as the term suggests, is the marriage of sound, video, graphics, animation, and text in computer applications by which one can present integrated representations. In the early 1990s, when multimedia was in its infancy, it was touted as a major means by which computer users could enhance communication. Today such applications are within the reach of the average user, both financially and in terms of ease of use. Common applications including PowerPoint, photo-editing programs, Web page development software, and others have brought the use of multimedia into all areas of computer use. In addition to a personal computer with a keyboard, multimedia may call for the use of microphones, speakers, sound recorders, headphones, digital cameras, scanners, and other devices for working with sound and video.

Multimedia applications have found their way into all computing environments. Home users enjoy entertainment multimedia, including gaming, virtual reality, music, and movies. Home users may also turn to multimedia software for planning meals, designing new homes, directing financial arrangements, shopping, and countless other uses. Home users are multitasking more often, using various applications for recreation at the same time, or listening to music while working on home projects.

In the workplace, multimedia designers followed the lead of entertainment applications and found many uses for multimedia. Business professionals are increasingly turning to presentation software such as PowerPoint for presentations and sales talks. Interactive Web sites are a must for businesses of every kind. Medical professionals find multimedia invaluable in diagnosing and treating patients, comparing notes and sharing information, and performing other important tasks. Designers, engineers, publishers, and representatives of almost any imaginable field turn to multimedia to assist in solving problems and presenting ideas. Training is also an area where multimedia is increasingly used. Multimedia in the workplace has dramatically changed how things are done and will continue to evolve.

Early uses of multimedia were for production of television shows such as *Sesame Street*. Here creator Chris Serf poses with characters used in the show's production in 1985. In the 1990s, multimedia production was within the capabilities of home users. (*Source: Infonautics in the U.S.A.* 16 (1985). Washington, DC: The United States Information Agency.)

Another area of use for multimedia is education. Whether the student is the youngest of children or a graduate researcher, there are applications to enhance learning for him or her. At their best, such programs go beyond the dreaded "drill and kill" to challenge learners to think creatively and critically. Students can demonstrate what they learn by creating Web pages, composing productions using multimedia applications, creating computer art, and expressing themselves in many ways. Multimedia offers an increasing number of tools for workplace productivity, home entertainment and utility, and educational applications. Every aspect of computer use will continue to be affected by the increasing sophistication in the evolution of multimedia.

BIBLIOGRAPHY

Cohen, S. and Rustad, J. (1998). "High-Tech\High-Touch: High Time?" *Training and Development,* 52 (December 1), pp. 30-36.

Robertson, G. (2002). "The Multimedia Advantage." *Billboard* 114 (April 6), p. 32.

Whatis.com (2002). "Multimedia." *Whatis?com's Encyclopedia of Technology Terms.* Indianapolis, IN: Que, p. 455.

Multitasking

Multitasking is a term that is fast becoming ubiquitous and refers to the ability to do more than one thing at once. People like to think of themselves as able to do this, but sometimes the results are questionable. Indeed, our fast-paced society has given rise to numerous warnings that people should slow down and do one thing at a time, avoiding the stress and increased errors that can result from human multitasking. With computers, though, multitasking is a good thing! When referring to computers, the term describes the operating system's ability to perform several operations simultaneously, likely using several programs to do so. Thus the user can listen to a CD while answering e-mail. At the same time another function could be ongoing, such as the downloading of data from an Internet source. The computer accomplishes this feat by switching from one program to another so quickly that the user perceives the functions as occurring simultaneously.

The idea of computer multitasking originated in the 1960s from multiple users seeking to utilize one mainframe computer. This early use, also called "time-sharing," was essential in the environment from which it sprang. From this origin, operating systems such as Windows and Mac OS sought to incorporate multitasking as a feature for the individual PC user seeking to complete several tasks at once. Most computers today employ a process called "preemptive multitasking," whereby each program in use is afforded a portion of operating time with the system preempting one process over another when an essential function, such as incoming data, must be completed. Modern operating systems have detailed provisions for prioritizing tasks.

Longtime computer users may remember the days when attempting to run more than one application at a time was likely to freeze the computer, lose data, or dramatically slow all processes. Today the speed at which multitasking can take place is such that thousands of processes can be completed in the time it takes a user to complete a couple of computer keystrokes. Nowadays the average user is likely to have several programs open at once. A user can copy or cut text or files from one, paste them into another, drag, drop, move about by clicking the taskbar or using the Alt and Tab keys. This flexibility, which we tend to take for granted, is far superior to having to save a piece of work, close the application, log onto the Web browser every time one wants to use it, then close it in order to transfer information into the desired application. Although jumping around from one task to another in personal work and play time may be inefficient, it is essential in computing.

BIBLIOGRAPHY

Margolis, P. (1999). "Multitasking." *Random House Webster's Computer and Internet Dictionary.* New York: Random House.

Nanny Cams

The mention of spy technology used to bring to mind movie thrillers such as the James Bond flicks, or clandestine operations by governmental agencies such as the CIA or KGB. It was the stuff of exotic locations, spies and spooks, and harrowing adventures. Today spy technology is finding its way into many homes and businesses. Internet Web sites sell spy gear such as hidden cameras and sound recording devices to the general public. Tiny cameras that can be hidden in smoke detectors, radios, stereos, and even books and stuffed toys are especially popular. They are sold legally for use in homes and workplaces, but the question arises as to whether they are then used legally. Laws about using cameras on job sites vary between states, and many people question the ethics as well as legality of filming employees and customers without their knowledge or consent. These concerns also apply to sound recording devices such as phone taps.

At the same time they are growing in popularity, partly due to accessibility and partly due to news coverage of some uses. Particularly newsworthy have been the revelations of nanny cams, placed in homes by concerned parents wanting to monitor how babysitters were treating their children while they were at work. In several cases, the camera revealed shocking scenes of sitters striking and verbally abusing children. Agencies such as Babywatch Corporation rent equipment to worried parents, whereas others opt to buy their own set-ups.

As with many new uses of technology, nanny cams are not without pitfalls or detractors. Invasion of privacy is a concern raised by some who say sitters may be fired for small infractions such as taking a break to watch television or making phone calls on the job. Others point out that the camera can catch only what happens in the room where it is located. If abuse is going on elsewhere, it will escape notice. Parents should trust their instincts rather than rely on electronic devices, advise some experts. Further, the devices may themselves put children and their families at risk. Individuals other than the intended recipients may intercept wireless video transmissions. Transmissions can easily be picked up by anyone cruising an affluent neighborhood where cameras are likely to be in place, using an inexpensive radio receiver. Thus someone could case a house for potential break-ins or even capture images of private moments for voyeurism or clandestine Internet publishing.

Despite the possible drawbacks, it is likely that home and workplace surveillance with cameras is a trend that will continue. Users and individuals who think they might be observed should be aware of both the positive and negative aspects of this technology.

BIBLIOGRAPHY

"Eye Spy . . . The Baby-Sitter!" (1996). *Time* 148 (July 22), p. 65.

Hamilton, T. (2002). "'Nanny' Cam Privacy Threat Exposed." *The Toronto Star* (June 14).

O'Malley, C. (1999). "Computers and Software: Internet: Spies Work the Web." *Popular Science* (June 1), p. 39.

Netiquette

Netiquette is nothing more than etiquette on the Internet. It comes from combining "network" and "etiquette." Although this seems simple enough, it has proven to be far more complicated than expected. Those who use the Internet often do not want what they input censored even if it is going to an electronic mailing list that may have thousands of members, some of whom may not appreciate the input or a particular remark. Because of the influx of diverse people using the Internet, netiquette is everchanging; however, most will say that Netiquette is based on the Golden Rule. Sometimes newbies to the Internet may need to follow examples to get a feel for what is or is not acceptable. *Netiquette* can also be defined as a code of conduct that governs what is generally considered to be the acceptable way for users to interact with one another online. Ross Shannon (2002) states that as in any public forum or culture, a collection of rules have developed over the years that govern how discussions are carried out on the Net. Sticking by them ensures a trouble-free time every time you connect to the Internet.

These rules should be known by anyone who's used the Internet for a while and should always be abided by. It is basic common sense. There may be a tendency on the Internet for abuse since people remain mostly anonymous. Misunderstandings are common occurrences. Emoticons are used to try to relay the feeling being expressed and this may help in preventing some misunderstandings. When entering a chat room or message board for the first time, take the time to learn the rules that may apply.

Moderators (those people chosen to keep order by dealing with troublemakers) can remove someone from the list because of cursing, rude remarks, hurting someone's feelings, etc. Some rules have more to do with the format being used. One such rule is: don't type everything in capital letters. In most forums this indicates shouting, so if you need to emphasize a point or actually want to shout, then use all caps, but use them sparingly. The other rule is to check for grammatical errors. Most programs have a spell checker, so use it before sending your message.

Just remember to use common sense, follow the Golden Rule, and learn the etiquette of the particular group with whom you are corresponding and your Netiquette will never be in question.

BIBLIOGRAPHY

Ecks, M. (2001). "Netiquette of Giving Feedback." Available from <http://writersu. s5.com/law/net1.html>.

Shannon, R. (2000). "Netiquette." Available from <http://www.yourhtmlsource. com/starthere/netiquette.html>.

Whatis.com (n.d.). "Netiquette." Available from <http://whatis.techtarget.com/ definition/0,,sid9_gci212635,00.html>.

New Economy

For thousands of years, humanity's economy was based on a transient nomad tribal system. The more animals a member could corral within the local village, the wealthier this member was. For thousands of years after that, humanity settled and developed the land in an agrarian economy. In this economy, the member who had the best tools had better luck taming the land, a better crop, more options in bartering, and so on. In the late eighteenth century, our economy began to develop into an industrial economy. More products were produced at a faster rate, requiring more skilled labor and better tools. Family farm-based agriculture began to slip away as more workers moved into the cities to fill the gap. Within the industrial economy, we had access to banks, shops, and stores in every neighborhood; on practically every corner. Ease of access to these services and convenience for the customer required even more products at even faster rates. Especially in America, we couldn't get our products fast enough. In all of this, the telecommunications infrastructure grew to meet the demands of this economy. Overnight, in the grand scheme, we became a "global village" (see GLOBALIZATION). With the advent of the Internet, consumers are able to bank, shop, purchase, and (in some cases) retrieve goods and services instantaneously around the world. This is our new economy.

The new economy is based on information technologies and telecommunications. Because of the serious decline in technology and telecommunications pricing in the early 1990s, small business and the average person now had access to the same kind of tools that megaconglomerate corporations had access to. This continued through most of the 1990s, when, it appears, the high-tech revolution didn't help firms or other forecasters anticipate changes in demand. Billions of dollars were invested in tech stocks and other ventures, and because the profit opportunities of the new technology companies, especially the dot-coms, were so difficult to gauge, valuations jumped to levels that often proved to be ridiculous. Amazon.com, for example, was worth billions during the first three years of its existence, though it had never seen a profit. With individuals it seems that the decline in equity valuations will result in a negative wealth effect. Consequently, spending will stay below income. As a result, some assert that the new economy is over. Others hold, however, that the new economy is not dead or even ailing. The new economy, whatever shape it's in, is still about globalization, information technologies, telecommunication, buying, and selling.

BIBLIOGRAPHY

Meyer, L. (2001). "A New Economy Again." *New Perspectives Quarterly* 18(4) (Fall), pp. 82-84.

New Media

Popular periodicals, ranging from business to technology, continually discuss new media. *New media* can be described as that which includes the use of traditional forms, i.e., text, audio, video, photography, and animation; with new forms: data, navigation, and nonlinear interactivity. New media, which is typically computer-based, electronic, and dynamic, does not obsolesce traditional media forms; rather, it allows everyone, from the smallest Internet broadcasters to megaconglomerate media companies to share content. With new media, broadcasters think in terms of users as opposed to viewers, while still maintaining the concept of a mass audience. New media forms are interchangeable and allow users to jump back and forth within the content, to like content, and to completely new content (including, but not limited to, hypertext and hypermedia). Simply put, new media is electronic communication.

Universities are looking to new media for use in education, via distance learning, to facilitate research, academic publishing, training, and for use in digital libraries. New media technologies offer and help facilitate collaboration, mutual criticism, and document sharing, utilizing hypertext, audio, video, interactive forms, and real-time discussion. Indeed, any sort of collaboration is available through the use of new media and new media technologies.

BIBLIOGRAPHY

Moxley, J.M. (2001). "New-Media Scholarship: A Call for Research." *Change* 33(6) (November/December), pp. 36-42.

Van Roekel, J.L. (2003). "Review of: *Digital Creativity: Techniques for Digital Media and the Internet,* by Bruce Wands." *Journal of the American Society for Information Science and Technology* 54(4), pp. 357-358.

Old methods of data storage, such as the 5¾ floppy disk pictured here, are all but obsolete with the advent of new media. (*Source: Infonautics in the U.S.A.* 6 (1985). Washington, DC: The United States Information Agency.)

Old Internet

The *Internet,* originally called ARPANET and sometimes simply called "the Net," is a worldwide system of computer networks through which people can communicate and obtain information. The history of the Internet began with the launch of the Soviet satellite Sputnik in 1957. The United States, eager to establish its lead in the race for military and scientific knowledge and technology, created the Department of Defense's Advanced Research Projects Agency (ARPA) in 1958. In 1962, Paul Baran, an electrical engineer who worked for the RAND (Research and Development) Corporation, was contracted by the government to study how the U.S. Air Force could maintain command and control over its nuclear arsenal and delivery systems following a nuclear attack. Baran's proposal was a decentralized military research network that operated via packet-switching, a system in which data are divided into smaller bits called *packets,* sent over a network (sometimes following different routes), and reassembled at their destination. According to some scholars, Baran was the first to develop the theory of packet switching; other scholars attribute the theory to Leonard Kleinrock, an emeritus professor of computer science at the University of California at Los Angeles. This theory formed the basis of Internet connections.

In 1968, ARPA contracted Bolt, Beranek, and Newman, Inc. (BBN), to create its military research network. The result was ARPANET, which came online in 1969. ARPANET was used initially, some believe, because of the difficulty to operate it, by computer experts, engineers, scientists, and later by librarians.

In 1972, Ray Tomlinson, an employee of BBN, created the first e-mail program. In 1974, the term *Internet* was coined. Many of the Internet's commands were standardized in the 1980s, making it easier for nontechnical people to use. This was especially true for e-mail— many university employees found e-mail to be an easy way to keep in touch with their colleagues at other institutions. The number of online sites exploded in the late 1980s, when many university libraries connected to the Internet. The number of hosts reached 100,000, but in just three years this number reached one million.

Released in 1992, the World Wide Web (WWW) made the Internet easier to navigate. In March 1991, the U.S. government lifted restrictions on commercial use of the Internet, paving the way for online business ventures. According to Cairncross (2001),

> Never has any new invention shot from obscurity to global fame in quite this way. In 1990, only a few academics had heard of the Internet. Yet by 2000, perhaps 385 million people around the world had acquired a new way to communicate, and a new global source of information on a giant scale. (p. 75)

BIBLIOGRAPHY

Cairncross, F. (2001). *The Death of Distance: How the Communication Revolution is Changing our Lives.* Boston, MA: Harvard Business School Press.

Howe, W. (2001). "A Brief History of the Internet." Available from <http://www.walthowe.com/navnet/history.html>.

Kristula, D. (2001). "The History of the Internet." Available from <http://www.davesite.com/Webstation/net-history.shtml>.

Zakon, R. (2003). "Hobbes' Internet Timeline." Available from <http://www.zakon.org/robert/Internet/timeline>.

Online Conferences

Online conferences utilize multimedia technologies in a Web-based, real-time broadcast with off-the-shelf software and hardware. Each site has a computer with an Internet connection, a small desktop video camera, computer microphone, speakers, and Internet conferencing software. Coordinators at each site dial an IP address much like dialing a telephone. After logging in, participants at each site receive video and text from the other sites on their screen while hearing conversations through their speakers.

Computers are required for Internet connection as well—this will continue to increase, as computers become general household appliances. As video compression improves, video quality and the decreasing use of bandwidth will make Internet videoconferencing a greater medium. The same is true for audio. In videoconferencing, the audio portion is by no means secondary to video. A good picture conveys greater communication. However, without a good audio signal, communication is more hindered than it would be with audio only—such as a telephone conversation. As these systems become increasingly integrated, and hardware and software costs plummet, individuals will have greater access to these systems and, consequently, utilize these systems to a greater extent.

Internet videoconferencing enhances the growth of international communication. In his book *Global Communication in Transition: The End of Diversity,* Hamid Mowlana (1996) contends that historically (i.e., in the twentieth century) international communication was initially viewed as propaganda; however, many saw this as an issue of education, cooperation, and interaction. He says that it is more important that specific value and belief systems embedded in human and cultural dimensions of international and societal relations be understood. Nicholas Negroponte (1995) reports that during the Gulf War, when international travel was banned, a gigantic growth in teleconferencing took place. Since then, computers have become equipped with low-cost telecommunications hardware. In this, computers will become increasingly "vision-ready."

Meaningful connectivity and communication technologies should be made available for everyone who wants them. Multimedia technology should be a monetarily sensible alternative to current applications. Multimedia technology becomes affordable as prices continue to drop. For less than $100, an individual who assumes ownership of or access to a computer with an Internet account can purchase a video camera, microphone, speakers, and software. Such trends are evident when reviewing popular literature, especially computer magazines of the past few years. This literature includes reviews and applications for such technology, while marketing the technology quite extensively.

BIBLIOGRAPHY

Mowlana, H. (1996). *Global Communication in Transition.* Thousand Oaks, CA: Sage Publications.
Negroponte, N. (1995). *Being Digital.* New York: Vintage Books.

Online Support Groups

Internet support groups or help groups have evolved as resources valuable to many individuals, and are embraced by many people as aids in facing and overcoming life's problems. The concept of support groups is not new; people have extolled for years the value of organizations such as Alcoholics Anonymous, Mothers Against Drunk Drivers, Weight Watchers, Parents Without Partners, and others. Now these and countless other groups are meeting in cyberspace. Whether groups are commercialized and well known or informal and known only to a few, members often credit them with playing vital roles in overcoming problems. In recent years, support groups have gone online, finding wide acceptance and interest. Online groups may share information by e-mail, instant messaging, online bulletin boards, chat, or combinations of e-communication modes. They boast several advantages over face-to-face groups. Participants can log on anytime and anywhere, thus eliminating the constraints of common times and locations for physical meetings. Contributors can use pseudonyms for identifying themselves, allowing for anonymity and privacy. People who face similar problems may be separated by hundreds or even thousands of miles and still share ideas and concerns, often with their different perspectives adding dimension to discussions.

Problems and challenges that bring people together online include health concerns, professional challenges, family problems, and psychological issues. A simple Internet search naming a problem, such as "heart disease," coupled with the term "support groups," is almost sure to bring up Web sites offering assistance. Many professions are well represented on the Web with support groups. Educators, librarians, technology support personnel, writers, and others can turn to online groups to compare notes, share ideas, and get answers to common questions.

As with other online agencies, support groups have downsides as well as benefits. Groups can degenerate into negativity if members resort to complaining rather than seeking improvement. Groups can also be sources of erroneous information thereby exacerbating the problems addressed. Sometimes support groups are frequented by unscrupulous individuals who pose as experts but have no background in the area of concern. These sites are also visited by people whose motives are not what they profess. One problem reported by certain medically oriented groups was that graduate students were visiting sites, posing as sufferers of various maladies and asking questions. They then took other members' responses and used them in research and class reports without asking permission.

When selecting a support group, it is a good idea to look for one that has reputable backing. Hospitals and clinics often sponsor medical discussion groups, and professional organizations frequently include such groups at their Web sites. The overall tone of communication can be another clue; it should be positive and supportive rather than negative or contentious. Steps should be in place to protect members' privacy. If the climate seems right and the information shared is verifiable, a support group can be very beneficial.

BIBLIOGRAPHY

Green, M. (2000). "New Teachers Find a Friend." *NEA Today* 19 (September), pp. 26-27.

Larkin, M. (2000). "Online Support Groups Gaining Credibility." *The Lancet* 355 (May 20), p. 1834.

Palm Computers or Personal Digital Assistants

Although some people prefer to keep their lives in line the "Big Chief" way (for those who may not remember, Big Chief was a brand of writing tablet once used by school children in the United States), many others have discovered the "Palm." *Palm* is the brand name for a line of personal digital assistants (PDA), handheld computers that are also known as palmtops (Whatis.com, 2002). PDAs are used mainly for personal organization, wireless e-mail, note taking, and electronic gaming. Most PDAs are approximately the size of a small calculator, and contain a microprocessor, operating system, memory, batteries, an LCD display, input and output ports, and software. They are capable of storing and processing data, as well as downloading and uploading information to and from the Internet. Information can be added to the PDA through a small keyboard, which is often available as a separate peripheral, or through a stylus, a penlike tool that can electronically write text, draw lines, or highlight information on the PDA's screen or a separate surface. A unique feature for many PDAs is their ability to recognize handwriting. Using a stylus, users can scan handwriting into the PDA, which is then converted to text. Some PDAs are better at recognizing handwriting than others.

One of the first PDAs was Apple's Newton MessagePad, which was criticized as being too big and too expensive. In 1996 Palm Computing introduced a new PDA called the PalmPilot, which proved to be extremely popular. In fact, PDAs are among the fastest selling consumer devices in history. One reason for their phenomenal sales record is that so many professions, including doctors, nurses, police, and government employees, have found uses for PDAs.

In the near future, PDAs are expected to include voice-recognition technology, built-in audio features, and smaller designs.

BIBLIOGRAPHY

Freudenrich, C.C. (n.d.). "How Personal Digital Assistants (PDAs) Work." Available from <http://www.howstuffworks.com/pda.htm>.

Jyotisoft (2002). "History of Palm." Available from <http://jyotishsoft.hypermart. net/pdahist.htm>.

Tam, P. and Pringle, D. (2003). "Hand-Held's New Frontier." *The Wall Street Journal* 242(28) (August 8), p. B1.

Whatis.com (2002). "Big Chief Tablet." *Whatis?com's Encyclopedia of Technology Terms*. Indianapolis, IN: Que, p. 71.

Whatis.com (2002). "Palm." *Whatis?com's Encyclopedia of Technology Terms*. Indianapolis, IN: Que, p. 515.

Peer-to-Peer File Sharing

Doesn't everyone learn in kindergarten to share with peers? As with other terms, *sharing* takes on a whole new meaning when applied to the world of the Internet. When describing computers and sharing, peer-to-peer architecture allows all connected hard drives to share as equals. Thus any user can access information and programs from any other computer to which he or she is connected. Although share and share alike may sound open and altruistic, it can lead to practices that have less than idealistic goals, with the most famous recent example being Napster.

Peer-to-peer (P2P) networks occur in cyberspace when users join together to use a "servent" application that turns each participant's PC into both a server and a client. Such applications can be downloaded free. One very popular free file-sharing application is Gnutella. After downloading the application, users share directly from one computer to another without going through a central server. Giving others access to one's hard drive sounds like an open invitation to hackers, but this threat is precluded by the fact that visitors can download from one's drive but cannot upload. There is the additional threat of viruses, though, and users should take appropriate protective steps.

Use of P2P networks presents several ethical and practical issues. Because of slow searches and downloads, they may put performance-draining burdens on computer servers. For this reason, universities, businesses, and other entities may bar their use. The issue of security is another concern. If a user on an individual machine poses a security threat, the entire network could be compromised. Further, as demonstrated in the Napster saga, copyright infringement is a considerable concern.

The controversy over P2P computing is here to stay, since the technology continues to proliferate. Business and publishing entities must become aware of the capabilities of peer-to-peer sharing and find ways to deal with the concerns it presents. Since peer-to-peer technology provides users with new ways to communicate and share in constructive endeavors, it offers great value as well as challenge.

BIBLIOGRAPHY

Arnold, S. (2001). "Journey to the Edge: Peer-to-Peer Computing and Content Control." *Searcher* 9 (October), pp. 64-74.

Grimes, B. (2001). "Can't Find That File? Try a Little Sharing." *PC World* (November), p. 57.

Portability

People in today's world are on the go. The days of growing up in one place and never straying far from that point of origin, or embarking on one career path and never straying, are in the past for most individuals. It is common in the United States to move a number of times and change jobs several times in the course of one's life. As people move about, they like to take with them the technological equipment that enhances their lives and increases productivity. Donald Norman (1998) refers to such appurtenances as "information appliances." They include devices for communication, imaging, information gathering, writing, printing, and many other functions. One common attribute that they share is an increasing priority on portability.

Anyone who doubts that people value portable technologies should visit an airport, mall, college campus, or other public gathering place. Here one will see people carrying and using various portable gadgets including pagers, phones, PDAs, laptop computers, CD players, medical tools, cameras, calculators, and others. It is not uncommon to see people carrying or wearing several portable devices, and using more than one simultaneously.

The availability of more portable information appliances will contribute to several trends regarding their evolution and use. One continuing priority is the drive for miniaturization. The device that seemed small and handy five years ago may be considered hopelessly bulky today. Chips and batteries are becoming smaller, allowing dramatic reduction in the size and weight of equipment.

In some cases, convergence is another important trend. Cellular phones may offer e-mail access, and will likely merge with other tools, such as word processors and day planners. According to Norman (1998), people will change their attitudes toward appliances, connecting them more to their interests and activities. Gear centered on specific activities such as music, sports, health, photography, personal finance, and other uses will increase in number and popularity.

People will have no qualms about buying equipment with very specialized functions. Thus, while one trend leads toward convergence, offering inventions that perform several functions, another trend is toward divergence, with specialized appliances gaining popularity as well.

Other changes involve how portable equipment is used and what it looks like. It is likely that more devices will be accepted as consumables. Throwaway cameras are already common, as are special-purpose consumables such as medical instruments for checking temperature, collecting blood, and other purposes. Communication among types of apparatus is likely to increase, as is already the case when someone synchronizes a day planner or PDA with a PC, or when a medical technician transfers information from a tool for monitoring a bodily function to a server.

The appearance of portable equipment and the ways people carry it are also expected to change. Voice recognition will diminish the need for keyboards. In *What Will Be,* Michael Dertouzos (1997) describes a world in which people will wear bodysuits. Bodysuits or body nets are already being pursued with envisioned capabilities to send everything from personal communication to medical data to the appropriate receiver.

This early laptop user enjoys computing while relaxing on his deck. (*Source: Infonautics in the U.S.A.* 38 (1985). Washington, DC: The United States Information Agency.)

In the future, eyeglasses will have communication capabilities embedded for transmitting and receiving both audio and visual experiences. Machines may be able to replicate everything that comprises one's perception of reality. Thus it may be possible to e-mail a friend, enjoy a TV show, and pay bills while taking a walk in the park.

The societal trend for people to be increasingly mobile is not likely to reverse. As they move through the stages of their lives, they will take technology with them in new and different ways.

BIBLIOGRAPHY

Dertouzos, M. (1997). *What Will Be.* New York: Harper.

Norman, D. (1998). *The Invisible Computer: Why Good Products Can Fail, the Personal Computer Is So Complex, and Information Appliances Are the Solution.* Boston, MA: MIT Press.

PowerPoint Poisoning

Not so long ago, audiences knew they were in for a long and boring session when a presenter fired up the trusty overhead projector and proudly displayed the first of many text-filled, hard-to-read transparencies. Nowadays a new player dominates this field: Microsoft's PowerPoint or one of its presentation software relatives. Audiences are greeted by the dimming of lights which places the focus on a screen rather than on the speaker. One of PowerPoint's familiar backgrounds appears, followed by a sequence of displays sporting billets, graphs, and charts. At one time a novelty whose features were enough to hold audience attention, the PowerPoint presentation is often now an occasion for inward or outward groans of boredom. This all-too-frequent occurrence was highlighted in a well-known *Dilbert* cartoon that may have coined the phrase "PowerPoint poisoning," in which an audience member keels over after seeing too many slides.

Actually, of course, PowerPoint is a useful application that can be the vehicle for outstanding presentations. The creator just needs to follow a few commonsense practices. Probably the biggest mistake presenters make is cramming too much text into the displays. Slides should not present every word that the speaker will say, but rather show key words and concepts. Further, when the speaker goes on to read word for word from slides, the results can be stultifying. Also, the size of the audience and size of the presentation room should be considered. Often the screen is too small and distant for people to see. Presenting in a dark room divorces the audience from the speaker and invites people to nod off rather than pay attention. Complicated or irrelevant graphs and charts can detract rather than enhance. The cliché "bells and whistles" can take on new meaning if the creator gets too caught up in the software's features, such as intrusive sound effects, flashy transitions, and meaningless animations.

If the software is used judiciously as a presentation aid rather than overshadowing the message, PowerPoint is an excellent tool. Coupled with a prepared and dynamic speaker, it often fulfills its promise.

When misused, as with any other tool, the results can be the opposite of the intended goal of offering an effective presentation.

BIBLIOGRAPHY

Garber, A. (2001). "Death by PowerPoint." *Small Business Computing* (April 1). Available from <http://www.smallbusinesscomputing.com>.
McNealy, S. (1997). "The Killer App." *Forbes* (December 1), p. 152.

Privacy

Just because most computers are used behind closed doors does not mean that others cannot see what is taking place. Surfing the Net is like walking down a public street. Web sites use small programs called "cookies" that are downloaded onto a computer hard drive to track the sites that the user visits and send this information to the Web site administrators. This is usually done for marketing purposes, but it would not take much to make this a malicious activity. Never send an e-mail that you do not want broadcast to the whole world. Junk e-mail, or spam, is the most common tool used to violate online privacy. Experts say that consumers should not respond to spam e-mail in any way, and especially not by clicking on the "to remove from list" links. More often than not, these links merely help the spammer confirm that your address is active.

New Internet browsers now allow users to turn cookies off, i.e., denying a cookie download when a user visits a site. This may cause the site to not be displayed, so browsers have incorporated an "ask me first" function. This function, which will also be used in other privacy areas, asks the user if it is okay to download a cookie from a visited site. This is worthwhile if the site is trusted. Likewise sending an e-mail is no different than sending a postcard through the mail. Pretty Good Privacy (PGP) is one of the oldest methods of protecting e-mail. PGP is an application that encrypts e-mail at the user's computer using the recipient's public key. When the recipient receives the e-mail, the software decrypts the message using a secret private key. Both parties must install PGP in order to read and send encrypted messages.

Shopping online presents the greatest risk. Web sites take personal information such as name, address, telephone numbers, and credit card numbers to use themselves or to sell to other operations, and sometimes this information is stolen from them. Although credit card companies will usually absorb unauthorized charges, users should be careful where they shop. As in the real world, we have to trust someone. We just need to make sure that we trust the sites we are giving our information to.

As this kind of activity becomes more prevalent, there is greater risk to privacy. Some users are willing to give up a little privacy for convenience. Now and in the future, technology will offer ways of protecting privacy just as it offers ways to steal it.

BIBLIOGRAPHY

Arrison, S. (2002). "How You Can Protect Your Privacy." *Consumers' Research Magazine* 85(2) (February), pp. 10-13, 24.
Brandt, A. (2001). "Who's Snooping on You?" *PC World* 19(9) (September), p. 49.
"Protecting Your Privacy." (2001). *Fortune* 142(12) (Winter), pp. 27-28.

Punched Cards

This early punched card was used with the Jacquard loom to control the patterns of weaving. (*Source: Artificial Intelligence, Amplifying the Mind* 5 [March, 1985]. Washington, DC: The United States Information Agency.)

Who has not heard of punched card ballots? These are the same cards that caused such an uproar in the 2000 presidential election. Where did these cards come from and how are they read?

Punched cards have been around since the late 1800s. Herman Hollerith is credited with inventing the standard punched card, but he actually got his idea from seeing similar cards being used to control Jacquard looms. It was Joseph-Marie Jacquard, a Frenchman, who had the idea of using holes punched in a card to better control the pattern a loom weaves. The first cards Hollerith designed were used to tabulate vital statistics by the New York City Board of Health; however, they are more noted for their use in the 1890 census.

These cards have remained the same dimension, 7-3/8" wide x 3-1/4" high, and have become the standard so that encoding is consistent. According to Douglas Jones (2002) the original code used for punched card data recording had only 240 distinct punch positions

This Jacquard loom incorporated the use of punched cards to standardize weaving patterns. Surely Jacquard had no idea how this technique would influence future technology. (*Source: Artificial Intelligence, Amplifying the Mind* 5 [March 1985]. Washington, DC: The United States Information Agency.)

per card, but in the early 1900s, a new standard card format was introduced with forty-five columns of round holes per card and twelve punch positions in each column (540 punch positions). In 1928, IBM, which was founded by Hollerith as the Tabulating Machine Corporation and later changed to International Business Machines, introduced the rectangular hole, eighty column format, almost doubling the amount of data that could be recorded on a card. By the mid 1930s, IBM was predicting that round-hole cards would soon be obsolete. The typical card processing applications from the 1890s to the 1950s did not require the use of computers.

In the 1960s punched cards were the accepted symbol of computing, but today they survive mainly in use as turnpike toll receipts and automatic voting systems. By 1990 the electronic voting machines were considered viable replacements for the card ballots, and by the 2000 election most voting districts were using the newer technologies.

BIBLIOGRAPHY

Baehne, G.W. (Ed.) (1935). *Practical Applications of the Punched Card Method in Colleges and Universities*. New York: Columbia University Press.

Jones, D. (2002). "Punched Cards: A Brief Illustrated Technical History." Available from <http://www.cs.uiowa.edu/~jones/cards/history.html>.

Maxfield & Montrose Interactive, Inc. (1997). "Hollerith's Punched Cards." Available from <http://www.maxmon.com/punch1.htm>.

"Punch Card Technology." (n.d.). Available from <http://www.seas.upenn.edu/~pws/EMX/punch.html>.

Quantum Computing

Computer technology fundamentally works as on/off switches. These switches are digits: 1s and 0s; 1s are on, 0s are off. In computerese these switchable binary digits are called *bits*. Quantum computing utilizes subatomic bits, or "qubits," that can exist as a 1 or a 0 or as both simultaneously. Quantum computers use quantum-mechanical interactions that allow amazing calculating power. The chief advantage of a quantum computer is that it can be in multiple states simultaneously, known as "superposition," while also simultaneously acting on each possible state. A quantum computer could therefore perform innumerable calculations in parallel using only one processing unit.

Large quantum computers can handle some of the most difficult computing problems, such as factoring numbers to break encrypted messages, deciphering in seconds what would take today's computers centuries. Quantum computers are extraordinarily difficult to build because they rely on exquisitely controlled interactions among fragile quantum states. The most powerful quantum algorithms, such as fast factoring, require an additional quantum feature in the mixture of the states of many subatomic particles. In this, it has been discovered that because light turns, it is well suited to true quantum computation. Theoretically, a full-power quantum computer can be built by sending individual photons through simple linear optical elements, such as beam splitters and phase shifters.

As this technology develops and evolves, perhaps one day computer users will no longer be required to "think outside the box." There will be no box.

BIBLIOGRAPHY

Collins, G.P. (2001). "Computing with Light." *Scientific American* 285(12) (August), p. 18.
Gershenfeld, N.A. and Chuang, I.L. (1998). "Quantum Computing with Molecules." *Scientific American* 278(6) (June), pp. 66-71.

Safe Rooms

The 2002 Hollywood thriller *Panic Room* featured Jodie Foster as a mother who sought refuge from intruders in a specially designed room that was supposed to withstand any threat. It turned out to not be so safe, of course, giving filmmakers lots of ways to scare viewers. In real life, there is a growing demand for safe rooms, possibly spurred on by the movie's popularity. Safe rooms used to be built to withstand fires or tornados, and still boast these protections but tend to add more. Kevlar lining in walls was first used in Israel to help make spaces blast proof and this feature is gaining popularity in the United States as well. Communication devices are considered important additions, and often include cellular equipment and even ham radios in case phone lines are cut. A self-contained power generator and an air filtration system for protection against biohazards are other desirable features. Rooms can start with a price tag of $10,000 to $15,000 for a closet-sized space. Naturally they can be more spacious and offer additional amenities with the price tag going up accordingly. Fears of home invasion, terrorist attacks, and other threats will continue to inspire demands for technology to preserve personal safety in the once taken-for-granted sanctity of homes.

BIBLIOGRAPHY

Fischetti, M. (2002). "Safety at a Cost." *Scientific American* 287 (August), pp. 86-88.

Search Engines

Search engines give people a way to organize the massive amount of information they find on the Internet so that it may be useful. It does little good to know the answer is "out there," if one does not know where or how to find it. That's the goal of search engines. An *engine* is programming jargon for a program that performs a fundamental or essential function. A search engine has three components: (1) a *spider,* or crawler, which goes to all sites and all pages to search what is being asked of it; (2) a program that creates an index of all those searched sites; and (3) a program that receives and compares the request before it returns the results to the searcher.

Search engine can also describe special programs containing algorithms. The best known usage of the term uses an algorithm to search indexes of topics. Some of the most used search engines are Google, Yahoo, and Lycos, although there are hundreds more. Billed as the Web's most comprehensive directory, the Open Directory Project, <http://dmoz.org>, indexes more than 597,200 sites in 89,340 categories thanks to its 11,500 volunteer editors. Some search engines are set up so that the user can request information in common everyday language, whereas others are more selective. Web searching tips are available on the Internet as well as a free daily newsletter called "SearchDay" from *Search Engine Watch,* <http://searchenginewatch. com/>, featuring Web search news, reviews, tools, tips, and search engine headlines from across the Web. This is one way to keep up with the latest information regarding search engines.

BIBLIOGRAPHY

Laisha, M. (1999). "The Open Directory Project: The Spirit of the Web." Available from <http://www.laisha.com/zine/odphistory.html>.

Sherman, C. (2002). "Search Engines." Available from <http://searchenginewatch. com/searchday/02/sd0924-se-showdown.html>.

Whatis.com (2002). "Search Engine." *Whatis?com's Encyclopedia of Technology Terms.* Indianapolis, IN: Que, pp. 631-632.

Shareware

The television cuts to a commercial. It's the "Video Professor," and he's asking you to try his instructional videos and computer software before you buy them. The concept of "try before you buy" certainly isn't new, but its application in the world of computers dates back to the early 1980s and the birth of *shareware* and *Freeware*.

Simply put, *shareware* is copyrighted software that is distributed free on a trial basis. If the user likes the program, he or she may pay for it later. Sometimes the program is incomplete (e.g., certain functions are disabled in the trial version) or lacks customer support until the full version is purchased. *Freeware,* on the other hand, is software that is normally provided at no cost.

In 1981, Andrew Fluegelman, a successful attorney from California, created a telecommunications program called PC-TALK. Fluegelman marketed the program by letting people use it for free and paying for it if they liked it. He called his software *Freeware* (which it technically wasn't), a term he later trademarked. Around the same time, Jim Button, an IBM employee from Washington, created a program named EASY-FILE, which he marketed by asking people to share the software with others and sending him a donation if the program proved beneficial (this was called *user-supported software*). The coincidental similarities between the two men's marketing methods were not lost on a user who was evaluating their software. The user mentioned the similarities to Button, who eventually contacted Fluegelman. In late 1982, the two men agreed to reference each other's software and set a voluntary $25 donation price. Button also changed his software's name to PC-FILE to complement Fluegelman's PC-TALK (Callahan, 2000).

In 1983, Bob Wallace, a former Microsoft employee, created a word-processing program called PC-WRITE and distributed it through his *shareware* concept. Wallace's marketing approach was similar to that used by both Fluegelman and Button, but instead of simply making a donation, users were also encouraged to share the software with their friends in return for a commission on sales.

This new method of selling software quickly caught on, and eventually a standardized name for the concept was sought. In 1983, a programmer and writer named Nelson Ford held a contest that let computer users decide which term to use (because "Freeware" was trademarked, it couldn't be used by anyone but Fluegelman). The users chose "shareware," which, with Wallace's permission, became the standard term. For their groundbreaking contributions, Fluegelman, Button, and Wallace are considered the founding fathers of shareware.

BIBLIOGRAPHY

Callahan, M.E. (2000). "The History of Shareware." Available from <http://paulspicks.com/history.asp>.

"Freeware." (n.d.). Available from <http://searchenterpriselinux.techtarget.com>.

"Shareware." (n.d.). Available from <http://searchVB.techtarget.com/sDefinition/0,,sid8_gci212977,00.html>.

Skins

Skins are graphic files that are used to change the appearance of a computer program without changing the program itself. This is akin to changing your cell phone cover or a Windows theme on your computer desktop. The most popular skins are for Internet chat programs, MP3 audio and media players, Internet browsers, and games. Skins are typically downloaded from the Internet and installed on the local computer. Several Web sites offer templates that allow users to design their own skins. Skins are also available for operating systems such as Linux.

As skins become more popular, there is no limit to what users will be able to personalize. Because skins and the templates used to create them are shared, they are often considered to be open source. *Open source* is computer code that programmers share to make software products better or fill a gap. Open source is free. Taken together, the programming and user interface is entirely customizable. This will lead to users creating their own software to use across many divergent devices. Several technology companies, including IBM, have already begun to realize this trend and the ensuing implications. These companies are also researching alternatives to costly licensing fees for operating systems such as Windows and Sun Microsystems' Solaris. Open-source software such as Linux is not governed by any single company, therefore IBM has given away 40 million dollars of its own software tools in the hopes that it will prompt a flurry of development involving open source software.

Because of the huge success of open source, this kind of collaborative computing, including skins, will continue to change the way users utilize technology.

BIBLIOGRAPHY

Ante, S.E. (2001). "Big Blue's Big Bet on Free Software." *Business Week* 3761 (December 10), pp. 78-79.

Whatis.com (n.d.). "Skins." Available at <http://whatis.techtarget.com/definition/0,,sid9_gci213718,00.html>.

Spamming

Most people get phone calls from telemarketers or "junk" mail, those advertisements, sweepstakes information, etc., that clog mailboxes. Well, e-mail is no different with its unwanted, unsolicited mail that comes via the Internet. As with regular mail, it seems once a person is placed on these lists, which multiply, it is very difficult to get off. Gaspar (2002) reports that spamming has become more than a nuisance; it is costing money by jamming the flow of e-mail traffic, hogging servers, and taking up staff time. According to Webster's, the term *spam* is derived from a *Monty Python's Flying Circus* sketch in which the word (the name of a canned meat produced by Hormel) is chanted repeatedly over the other dialogue. When two lawyers sent an e-mail to thousands of message boards in 1994, the repetitious act led some to call it "spam." Thus spam became synonymous with unsolicited and/or unwanted e-mail (Templeton, n.d.).

Some sites give you an option to receive spam e-mails, but as with many legal documents, the option may be in fine print that does not get read or in some it is preselected by default. This obscure placement of information is actually known as a *spam trap*. Another term closely related to this is *spamdexing*. This is done by including a key word several times so that the search engine will think it is a more important term and index the information thusly. However, after reading the information, one can determine that the key word is not relevant to that information. Some will also include words that are totally unrelated, or will list a well-known person who has no relation to the information, just to get people to visit the site. Conry-Murray (2002) states that networks can take countermeasures to combat spamming. His suggestions for dealing with spam include: ignore it and let users delete the information themselves; complain to the Internet service provider; develop software that filters the e-mail; or file a lawsuit. An acronym, S4L, stands for "spam for life," and with some online services this is what you get.

BIBLIOGRAPHY

Conry-Murray, A. (2002). "Spam Smackdown—From Filtering E-Mail to Filing Lawsuits, Network Administrators Have an Arsenal of Weapons for Wrestling Spam." *Network Magazine Incorporating Data Communications* 17(5) (May 1), pp. 62-66.

Gaspar, S. (2002). "Fighting Back Against Spam—There's No Silver Bullet, But a Coordinated Strategy That Includes Usage Policies, Antispam Tools and Services Can Greatly Reduce Spamming." *Network World* 19(19) (May 13), pp. 48-50.

Livingston, B. (2002). "Spam War Escalates—Windows Users Have a Choice Between Questionable and Effective Ways to Stop Unwanted E-Mail." *InfoWorld* 24(24) (June 17), p. 23.

Templeton, B. (n.d.). "Origin of the Term 'Spam' to Mean Net Abuse." Available from <http://www.templetons.com/brad/spamterm.html>.

Whatis.com (2002). "Spam." *Whatis?com's Encyclopedia of Technology Terms*. Indianapolis, IN: Que, p. 669.

Technophobia

Computer technology is embraced by many as a wonderful boon, a means of enhancing productivity and enriching life in countless ways. Some individuals, however, view technology as a terrible bane—the source of frustration, confusion, and stress. For these people, the prospect of using a computer results in consternation rather than celebration. The terms "technophobia" and "technostress" have been coined to describe this malady. People with a pronounced antipathy for unfamiliar devices or computer applications are said to be technophobic. Books have been written on the topic, classes offered, support groups organized, and still the condition exists. Some sufferers even exhibit physical symptoms of stress when confronted with new technologies. The antidote is training offered by sympathetic and understanding leaders who help people overcome their fears, coupled with honest and determined efforts by victims. As with most fears, technophobia rises from a fear of the unknown.

Technophobia can affect the atmosphere of the workplace, school, or any environment where technology is in place and people need to use it to conduct routine activities. In the workplace, lack of confidence and ability to use computers can impede performance. Ignoring the situation may lead to loss of productivity, increased absenteeism, and low morale. Sometimes people are afraid to even turn on equipment or complete simple tasks for fear of breaking something or losing valuable information. The fact that youngsters often know more than these adults do about computers and technology also bothers some technophobes.

Trainers can do a great deal to allay the fears of people who find technology stressful by offering assistance in a nonthreatening manner. Such training should be hands-on with plenty of reassurance for neophytes that they are not likely to damage anything and that they can succeed in completing the tasks presented. Repeated success, small steps, and ongoing encouragement are essential. Often pairing a new user with a more experienced and understanding colleague is a helpful ploy. For many reluctant users, learning how to communicate with family and friends via e-mail is the entree to learning any number of other processes. Using humor is another valuable training technique.

Currently the two greatest fears Americans acknowledge are public speaking and death. If adequate training is offered and people suffering from fear of technology acknowledge their problem and allow themselves to learn, technophobia will not end up topping this list of fears.

BIBLIOGRAPHY

Snyder, D. and Culp, J. (1997). "Training Technophobes." *Training and Development* 51 (September), pp. 12-13.

TWAIN

"Technology without an important name." This is what some claim TWAIN stands for, although others say it is not an acronym. TWAIN is a program that lets one scan images directly into an application program for manipulative uses. Without this program, one would need to close any open application, open a special program to get the image, and move that image to the program where one intended to use it. This process is time-consuming and impractical. It is also inefficient to ask that a software company develop a program for every device it might be used with, nor to ask the hardware companies to write a different program that could accept any software program. Users need some compromise or some standard for this to be a viable program.

In the early 1990s, the TWAIN Working Group was formed. Its members included representatives from both the software industry and the hardware industry. These members had to work together to provide a solution to this problem, combining diversity and unity. The group stated that its purpose was to produce a standard software protocol and application programming interface for communication between software applications and image acquisition devices. After many meetings, input from various sources, and using the best of products already available, TWAIN was developed. Now TWAIN is included with most scanners and is the industry standard.

BIBLIOGRAPHY

Hewlett Packard (1997). "HP Scanjet Scanners—What Is TWAIN? Definition and History." Available from <http://www.hp.com/cposupport/scanners/support_doc/bps01512.html>.

The TWAIN Working Group (2003). "About TWAIN." Available from <http://www.twain.org/about.htm>.

Whatis.com (2002). "TWAIN." *Whatis?com's Encyclopedia of Technology Terms.* Indianapolis, IN: Que, p. 740.

URL

What is your URL? This seems to be a common, frequently asked question these days. What is being asked? It is your Internet address. A uniform resource locator (URL) is a file address that is accessible on the Internet. A resource can be an image file, an HTML page, or any other file that is supported by HTTP. A URL must contain three components. It must have the name of the protocol, which is the set of rules the computer follows in order to communicate with another computer. The URL lets the computer know how to process the information it receives. The URL must contain the domain name that identifies a specific computer on the Internet and a hierarchical description of a file location on that computer. A URL is then a type of URI, or uniform resource identifier. This represents a standardized way of specifying the addresses not only of Web pages, but files, newsgroups, and even e-mail users.

An example of an address would look like this: <http://www.shsu. edu>. The *http://* is called the "protocol type identifier"; it also identifies the document as a Web site. The *dot* joins each element of the address and gives it a unique identifier. The *domain name* is also unique. Usually in giving an address it will be stated as dot-com or dot-edu, in this case, which indicates that the page is registered to a commercial user or to an institution, in this case, an educational institution.

It also takes a browser to get from the address to the actual site. The browser must communicate with the server, obtain permission to access the site, and then actually load the site onto your server. The browser serves other functions as well.

Sites that add and update URLs serve as indexes. There are also sites that will help users develop a personalized Web site. It seems that most people want dynamic, even interactive Web sites, so when others access the URL it will be appealing as well as informative.

BIBLIOGRAPHY

Anderung, L. (2003). "Uniform Resource Locator." Available from <http://www.uibk.ac.at/info/kurs/htmlkurs/htmlref/url.html>.

Google.com (n.d.). "Share Your Place on the Net with Us." Available from <http://www.google.com/addurl.html>.

Shipman, J. (2000). "What is a URL (Uniform Resource Locator)?" Available from <http://www.nmt.edu/tcc/help/html/url.html>.

Whatis.com (2002). "URL." *Whatis?com's Encyclopedia of Technology Terms.* Indianapolis, IN: Que, pp. 751-752.

Usenet

Usenet is a globally distributed discussion system. It consists of newsgroups covering practically every conceivable topic. Articles are posted to a newsgroup by computer and Internet users using news software, usually found within an e-mail program. Many newsgroups are moderated in that the articles are sent to a moderator for approval prior to posting. Newsgroups often allow questions to be submitted and answered by subscribers to the group. These groups may be limited to certain servers and networks, but most are available over the Internet. Thousands of subscriptions are available. Subscriptions are organized by newsgroup hierarchies. The most utilized hierarchies are comp (computers), rec (recreation), sci (science), soc (society), and news. Newsgroups fall into categories under these headings. An example of a newsgroup is <rec.photo.equipment.35mm>. It is obvious that this newsgroup discusses 35mm photographic equipment.

An inherent difficulty with newsgroups is reliability. Although many groups are moderated, this does not necessarily mean that the information posted is authoritative. It may be good information, but one's credentials are not usually listed with the post. This may be less of an issue in recommending a camera for a trip than a medical procedure, but readers should be aware that these are public forums accessible from all over the world. Another issue with Usenet is its size. With thousands of groups and thousands of messages, it may take an exorbitant amount of time to search or peruse, though Internet search engines are helpful in this respect. Deja.com, for example (soon to be a part of the Google search engine) archives and indexes Usenet and other newsgroups. As with any search engine, simply type a request into the search window. If the search engine returns too many matches, add more specifics to the search string; if too few matches are returned, broaden the search by reducing the number of required terms.

BIBLIOGRAPHY

Spanbauer, S. (2000). "Explore and Survive the Usenet Jungle." *PC World* 18(4) (April), pp. 236-237.

"Usenet Help." (n.d.). Available at <http://www.ibiblio.org/usenet-i/usenet-help. html>.

Virtual Reality

Some people are visionaries; others are not. Some individuals, who fall into the latter category, may wonder where furniture, appliances, etc., would fit when building a new house or moving to an apartment. What if engineers who are designing a new car could sit in the car and get a feel for where to place controls? *Virtual reality,* a term coined by Jaron Lanier, will allow this to happen. According to Whatis.com (2002),

> Virtual reality is the simulation of a real or imagined environment that can be experienced visually in the three dimensions of width, height, and depth, and that may additionally provide an interactive experience visually in full real-time motion with sound and possibly with tactile and other forms of feedback.

This can be accomplished by using head-mounted display, bodysuit, and glove. One could use this program to feel as though he or she were actually in a room to arrange furniture or appliances for best fit before physically moving one piece. The ability of the program to zoom in or out and move the objects from place to place helps with the reality perception.

As with many of our technology advances, virtual reality came about because the U.S. military wanted to develop a radar system that could display information service members could readily understand. This system had to be able to process large amounts of information quickly. The result was instantaneous simulation of data—the first use of virtual reality. The government also found it cheaper to train pilots on the ground, which resulted in flight simulators being developed. As technology became more advanced the images projected became more lifelike.

Technology wizards, especially those in the entertainment industry, also became interested in the implications of virtual reality. One can see this in the movies that have been released in the past decade.

Many other uses for virtual reality have become viable, with its potential not fully realized particularly in the medical profession. With virtual reality, doctors can simulate the experience of a surgical procedure prior to undergoing the real thing. The field is still wide open. Iowa State University (2002) reported that it had conducted forty-seven virtual reality projects in the 2001-2002 school year alone.

Virtual reality will change the way we interact with the computers of the future. Its future will be limited only by our imaginations.

BIBLIOGRAPHY

Iowa State University (2002). "2001-2002 Annual Report: Virtual Reality Applications Center." Available from <http://www.vrac.iastate.edu/about/AnnualReport2002/ProjectsPages/Projectspage.htm>.
University of Illinois (1995). "Virtual Reality: History." Available from <http://archive.ncsa.uiuc.edu/Cyberia/VETopLevels/VR.History.html>.
Whatis.com (2002). "Virtual Reality." *Whatis?com's Encyclopedia of Technology Terms*. Indianapolis, IN: Que.
World Future Society (1999). "Doctors May Feel Their Patients' Pain." *The Futurist* 33(1) (January 13), p. 13.

Viruses

One thing that can strike dread in the heart of a dedicated computer user is the threat of viruses. The very word, which conjures up images of human suffering, is enough to cause anxiety. A computer virus is actually a computer program, but one whose purpose is malicious rather than benign or beneficial. Most often a computer virus is a small program that attaches itself to programs already residing in and essential to a computer's hard drive. Viruses usually attach executable files that operate various computer functions, often going after files in the boot sector (files that are called upon to start up the computer).

Sometimes the resulting actions are relatively harmless, such as a "gotcha" message appearing on the screen that is more scary than serious. Other viruses, however, can destroy or damage data or even bring down the entire computer operating system. Many computer users are unsure how viruses are spread and how to protect against them. Viruses are spread via floppy disks, computer networks, or Internet access. Contrary to ongoing rumors, a virus cannot be contracted simply by opening an e-mail message. If the message recipient opens an infected attachment, though, the virus can then be transmitted.

Viruses are unpleasant at best and destructive at worst, so it is wise to practice safe computing in order to avoid them. Several common-sense measures should be kept in mind. First, remember that viruses cannot destroy computer hardware, only software. Therefore the wise user will keep up-to-date and readable backups of all programs and files. Second, it is never a good idea to download a file without knowing for sure that it comes from a safe and reliable source. It is not safe to download from Internet sources that are not well established and reputable, nor is it advisable to open e-mail attachments or files unless the sender is equally trustworthy. Finally, no computer should be without a virus protection program. A number of excellent software packages are available for virus protection. Once a user has installed a program, he or she should make sure that it is maintained with the latest upgrades and updates.

Because viruses engender fear and even panic, they are tempting to mischief makers who enjoy spreading hoaxes as much as spreading actual viruses. It is not uncommon for a virus threat to spread like wildfire, often through dire e-mail messages that start with the pronouncement, "This is not a hoax!" A good idea that can defuse such panic is to check the facts, certainly before forwarding the message to others and thus feeding the hoax. Internet sites, including those hosted by virus protection software companies and other independent concerns, can supply the truth. While viruses are troublesome and potentially damaging, they can be avoided by the conscientious practice of avoidance procedures readily available to all users.

BIBLIOGRAPHY

Komando, K. (1998). "When Your Computer Gets Sick." *Popular Mechanics* 175 (September 1), pp. 72-76.
Whatis.com (2002). "Computer Virus." *Whatis?com's Encyclopedia of Technology Terms*. Indianapolis, IN: Que.

Voice Activation and Recognition

In the twenty years since computers began to talk, in their "synthesized, metallic voice," which no one would mistake for a human voice, the past five years have seen great advancement. The distinction between the computer voice and the "real thing" is difficult to distinguish. However, the greatest challenge is not from text to voice, but from voice to concept and expression. Getting a computer to handle context is a high challenge.

Speech-recognition systems are either speaker-dependent or speaker-independent. In the first, the system learns to recognize the user's or speaker's voice. In the independent system, the program responds to the word no matter who is speaking.

The newest software can perform speech recognition independently in a stand-alone mode, recognizing up to fifteen words or phrases, or it can function as a slave under a host processor, recognizing up to sixty words. "When the module hears a word that it's been trained to recognize, it then outputs a digital signal corresponding to the word recognized" (Iovine, 2000, p. 55).

In the near future we will be interacting with "smart gadgets" by speech through voice activation. Today's market reveals only the "tip of the buy" for the future. We will no doubt be able to answer a knock or doorbell, though not at home, through voice and video.

Speech recognition in humans involves the ears, auditory stimulation, and the linguistic center of the brain; it also involves memory, which is very important in computers as well. Both humans and computer will need to know something about semantics—language structure and context all contribute to recognition. Humans have all the necessary components; computers have a way to go.

Several approaches to speech recognition have been used. Pattern matching was one method used during the 1970s. The program's major weakness was that it was better at recognizing its "trainer" than it was for general application. Another more recent approach is neural networking, which attempts to emulate the structure of the brain in comparing what is being said to how it is being said. *Fuzzy logic* is yet another approach to speech recognition. This approach is associated with the mathematical theory of uncertainty. It is similar to the neural network in that even though a computer may be able to interpret words, it cannot, at this time, interpret the many nuances humans use when communicating. Computers still lack the ability to put it all together and arrive at the understood response, since voice or speech recognition is simply the *ability* of the computer to interpret dictation.

BIBLIOGRAPHY

Iovine, J. (2000). "'Wrecking Nice Beaches' with Voice Recognition." *Poptronics* 1 (October), p. 55.

Saracco, R., Harrow, J.R., and Weihmayer, R. (2000). *The Disappearance of Telecommunications.* New York: IEEE Press.

Whatis.com (2002). "Voice Recognition." *Whatis?com's Encyclopedia of Technology Terms.* Indianapolis, IN: Que, p. 774.

Wearable Computing Devices

Miniaturization and portability of computerized devices has given rise to a number of gadgets, including PDAs, that can be carried or worn like clothing or even implanted. Proponents of wearables state that today's computers, which are bound to a static location such as a desk, and laptops do not fulfill the promise or potential of computers. Making computer applications available through items such as eyeglasses or clothing would increase flexibility and enhance use. A wearable device should be able to interact with the user within the context of a given situation. Despite sounding like something from a James Bond movie, such equipment is moving into the world of reality. DARPA, the United States' Defense Advanced Research Projects Agency, has issued a call for proposals for computer systems made of fabric. Such e-textiles could be used as global tracking instruments or solar power generators, or they might be worn as clothing or used to cover military vehicles and equipment.

Today's market already includes some wearable gear, such as wrist-top PDA and mobile phones, MP3 players powered by body heat, eyeglasses that translate signs from one language to another, smart ID tags and badges, medical equipment that can be worn to monitor bodily functions, and smart sneakers that can monitor movement for use by therapists or athletic trainers. Companies such as FedEx are using wearable computers for use by inspectors and technicians, with voice recognition and hands-free operation. Medical developments offer the promise of innovations such as the artificial eye, implanted devices to monitor and administer insulin to diabetics, and others. A London developer has even proposed production of a bra that includes a global positional apparatus and a phone to provide the wearer with a way to call for help in case of an attack.

What will it take to move wearable computers into the mass market? Clearly the promise of popular use is in the near future. Popular clothing manufacturers such as Levi Strauss are planning items such as jackets with MP3 players in special pockets and embedded GSM mechanisms. Xybernaut, a company that specializes in wearable computing devices, boasts such products as Poma, a wearable multimedia and computing appliance, and Xyberkids, and backpack/ computer for youngsters. Such gadgets are going to be expensive at first but should decline in cost with increased production and demand. It is up to the consumer to drive this wave of development by adopting the products and demanding more. Doubtless as technology and miniaturization continue to evolve, these early inventions will be refined and will grow into more sophisticated tools that seem beyond our collective imagination today.

BIBLIOGRAPHY

"The Future Me." (2001). *PC Magazine* 20 (September 4), p. 185.

Lewis, J. (2001). "Put on Your Human-Machine Interface." *Design News* 56 (August 20), pp. 48-50.

Merritt, R. (2001). "Switching Fabric." *Electronic Engineering Times* 1191 (November 5), pp. 1-3.

Xybernaut Corporation (2003). "Technology That Works with You." Available from <http://www.xybernaut.com>.

Webcams

A graduate student trains a camera on his workspace and invites friends and even strangers to "drop by" his Web site and wish him well as he slaves away on his dissertation. If a visitor signals him, he will smile and wave. Another webcam enthusiast specializes in showing images of himself and others as they sleep. Still another devotee is never without her wearable camera, which broadcasts everything she does and everything that happens to her. With today's penchant for reality in television programming, it is no surprise that webcams are popular. They perform the same function as surveillance or spy cameras, with the notable difference being the fact that the person viewed is the willing instigator and subject.

What are the mechanics behind these and other cinematic Web ventures? Generally a small and unobtrusive device, a webcam, digitally captures images and distributes them via an Internet site. Today a webcam costs less than $50 and can be set up with ease. Sometimes multiple cameras are used, offering views of several rooms in a house. The earliest pioneers in this realm included offerings such as the "Fish Cam," which shared continuously the lives of fish in a bowl, or the "coffee cam," which was trained on an automatic coffeemaker. The very first webcam was the Trojan Room Coffee Cam, which originated at the Cambridge University Computer Laboratory in 1991. The second oldest webcam, the "Fish Cam," was founded by Netscape originator Lou Montulli around 1995, and was said at one time to be one of the ten most popular sites on the Internet. The popularity of such mundane presences revealed the interest that people have in watching things unfold from afar.

One of the most famous personalities to emerge from this milieu is Jennifer Ringley of "Jennicam fame." Her webcam has captured and broadcast all the at-home moments of her life since 1999. Like many webcam subjects, she is a young female. Much of her time is spent at home, and she reports feeling quite comfortable living her life before a camera. Many subjects report that they like to think of viewers as "guardian angels" rather than "peeping toms." Webcam sites typically bolster the viewer's knowledge about their owners by supplying profiles of themselves, diaristic writings, galleries of still pictures, and other additions. Often viewers are invited to leave messages or chat.

Private lives become public and viewing becomes a continuous opportunity rather than a static event of prescribed duration. The person being watched has control over what the watcher is allowed to see, though frequently little is restricted. Certainly webcams offer a new and emerging type of communication, if not artistic genre.

BIBLIOGRAPHY

"The Amazing Netscape Fish Cam." (n.d.). Available from <http://fishcam.netscape.com/fishcam/>.

Knight, B. (2000). "Watch Me! Webcams and the Public Exposure of Private Lives." *Art Journal* 59 (Winter), pp. 21-25.

McCracken, H. (2001). "Reach Out and See Someone." *PC World* 19 (April), pp. 35-37.

"The Trojan Room Coffee Machine." Available from <http://www.cl.cam.ac.uk/coffee/coffee.html>.

Webquests

The ever-increasing presence of computers and Internet access in schools has challenged educators to develop the best practices possible for using technology to enhance learning. Bernie Dodge, a professor of educational technology at San Diego State University, originated the term *Webquest* to describe an activity designed to help students learn from electronic and print informational resources. The key element of a Webquest is that it calls upon students to solve a problem or answer a question. In order to solve the problem, they must dissect information related to the question, usually from the Internet and library resources. A well-constructed Webquest should have a clearly stated task at the beginning, offering Web links and other information about where to find useful materials. Often students are called upon to work in teams to locate, gather, and evaluate pertinent information. Team members may be assigned roles describing their duties during the activity. Gathered information should then be used to reach a solution to the original problem or answer the question first presented. Finally students should evaluate the information and their work as well as their final solution. After students become adept at solving Webquests, they can design their own, an activity that further develops their abilities to think critically and evaluate information.

Because Webquests inspire critical thinking and require students to analyze and evaluate information, they are popular activities for schoolteachers and librarians. The best source of information about Webquests is Bernie Dodge's *The WebQuest Page* <http://Webquest. sdsu.edu/Webquest.html>. Activities such as Webquests enable students to go beyond the drill-and-practice instruction frequently offered by computer learning software applications.

BIBLIOGRAPHY

Braun, L.W. (2001). "In Virtual Pursuit." *Library Journal* 126 (October 15), p. 32.

Dodge, B. (n.d.). *The WebQuest Page at San Diego State University.* Available at <http://Webquest.sdsu.edu/Webquest.html>.

Wired Environments

A *smart home* is one that includes computerized technology to enhance the inhabitants' lifestyle in as many ways as possible. Such environments are wired to perform a number of tasks automatically or conveniently upon command. It is difficult to pinpoint a year that could be called the inception point of such technology, since evolution has been slow and ongoing, but the nomenclature has been used since the early 1990s. New home construction will likely incorporate smart features incrementally, until such features are the norm rather than novelty.

Common features at this time offer conveniences, security, entertainment, etc. Systems such as lighting, burglar alarms, and climate controls can be programmed automatically in many homes. This can be governed by preprogramming or by sensors placed throughout the home that determine when a given action should initiate.

Some homes offer more sophisticated functions. For example, a busy mother can check the contents of her kitchen's refrigerator and pantry from work, if they are equipped with optical scanners that can read product bar codes. Upon determining what is on hand, she can signal her oven to preheat or perform other tasks to prepare for her arrival. She can also govern her home sprinkler system or thermostat in order to make adjustments for weather changes. A smart home can simulate the activities carried on during normal routines while occupants are out of town. Apartment complexes are also getting into the act, and those offering wired environments report that the resulting features are viable selling points.

The advantages of smart houses go beyond convenience and novelty. Safety is of paramount concern to many homeowners who are attracted by the growing options for enhancing home security, fire and other disaster alerts and aids, etc. Family members, especially parents with small children, can keep tabs on one another via updated intercom and video monitoring systems. Proponents of smart houses say they can save energy by turning devices on only when they are needed, and regulating thermostats to avoid excessive climate control costs.

Features that are currently in use by early adopters include wiring a house as a LAN (local area network), so that networking is available in every room. Entertainment features might include state-of-the-art DVD and CD players that can be accessed throughout the house, governed by remote controls. Software could sense entry when one returns home and automatically start a meal or turn on favorite music. New appliances may include diagnostic chips that can allow a repairman to fix them remotely, or at least diagnose the problem and bring the necessary parts to complete a repair. One company is proposing a smart mirror that would allow one to access the Internet while shaving or putting on makeup in the morning. There is even a smart toilet with a monitoring device that can ship relevant data to health care providers via the Internet.

How and when will the technology that makes a dwelling a "smart house" be implemented? New homes with numerous features are increasingly common, with packages adding around $10,000 to the price. The infrastructure, or wiring within the walls of the building, is best put into place during construction. Aspects of the technology can be assimilated into any home. Starting points might be a home security system or an entertainment module.

Is there a downside to the evolution of smart environments? Cost is a barrier to many potential users at this time, but is expected to decrease with increased demand and production. Privacy is a growing concern, and much of the information thereby generated would by necessity flow via the Internet. The ability to protect users' privacy will continue to be a challenge and a concern. Furthermore, the threat of a pervasive virus with the potential to disable all these wonderful smart features is a consideration. Potential solutions to these problems exist, but they will likely call for international agreements before they are solved, according to Vinton Cerf, senior vice president at MCI WorldCom (Cerf, 2000). Finally, because such devices will be networked, the smart home will only be as reliable as the network that supports it. If the home network goes down, one will be faced with the resulting inconvenience. Despite the challenges, it seems likely that wired environments are here to stay.

BIBLIOGRAPHY

Cerf, V. (2000). "Visions 21/Our Technology: What Will Replace the Internet?" *Time* (June 19), pp. 102-105.
"Digital Domiciles." (2001). *PC Magazine* 20 (February 6), p. 133.
Levy, S. (1999). "The New Digital Galaxy." *Newsweek* 22 (May 31), pp. 56-62.
Perritano, J. (1999). "High IQ Homes." *Current Science* 85 (September 24), pp. 4-7.

Wireless Application Protocol

Wireless. Everyone is talking about it. Who can carry the smallest device with the most options and greatest access? Wireless technologies, though nothing new, are becoming more and more prevalent. Readers of practically any business or computer magazine will find quite a bit of content and advertisements regarding mobile telecommunications. These periodicals are typically geared to both office-based and home-based users. Satellite technology, mobile computing, paging, e-mail, and telephone services are becoming more prevalent and less expensive. These devices include mobile phones, palm devices, and mobile PCs. Using microbrowsers, these devices are able to download wireless application protocol (WAP) documents formatted in wireless markup language (WML) for viewing on a portable screen. Because of the rather small screen on most wireless devices (some are one inch square), it is important to maximize content in a minimalist way.

Many complain about the problems with WAP: It is slow, full of security holes, the devices are tiny, and the same information may be found in a newspaper. My cell phone uses WAP and it's lousy. Finding information takes forever. But it fits in my pocket, and I'm going to carry it with me anyway. WAP shines in its ability to show us where we are heading. It is forcing companies to agree upon standards—already a nonissue in Japan and Europe.

Internet-connected phones are here to stay. These devices offer personalized information content, such as stock quotes, weather, movie times, news, restaurant guides, driving directions, etc. Users can trade stocks, buy a book, book a flight, and access bank accounts. WAP allows users to synchronize their e-mail, calendars, address books, and to-do lists wirelessly over the Internet. Some ventures have been made into using wireless devices to buy junk food from vending machines, in which the machines charge an account through the WAP device.

BIBLIOGRAPHY

"The Internet Unplugged." (2001). *Fortune* 142(12) (Winter), pp. 160-162.

Wireless Networks

Wireless networks are everywhere. They allow us to leave the desk, to leave the corporate ground, and still be at work. Once, in landline days, we could escape the network, but today no one seems to want to escape—they relish taking it with them. More and more people want to keep in touch with information no matter where they are. This demands that wireless networking continues to improve and is made available to more and more people, especially those in the developing countries.

According to Cairncross (2001), "Many developing countries will use new technology to race into the new century" (p. 15). They will build wireless networks because this is cheaper and faster. It takes a decade to repair a road from Nairobi to Mombassa and even longer to clear landlines for all those in Nigeria who want phones. Some African countries now have more mobile than fixed connections, and e-mail is now the method of communication in many parts of Africa. Mobile phones provide great service, and are getting better as technology advances. For instance, the Star-TAC phone by Motorola first reflected what miniaturization could accomplish, and "eventually circuitry can be woven into fabric itself" (Saracco, 2000, p. 144). We are truly living in a connected world.

One of the great assets of the wireless network is, or rather must be, remote surgery. In developing countries the need for such services is great. What a miracle it would be if wireless networks could provide surgeons with a 3-D view of patients and their medical needs. To be able to get medical help from thousands of miles away will be truly one of the greatest contributions wireless networking could make to our society.

Wireless communication brings fundamental changes to data networking and telecommunications, and makes integrated networks a reality. *Wireless Networks,* the journal, focuses on networking and user aspects. Wireless connections can also be customized for individual users and are very good for the economy. According to Gast

(2002), however, there *is* a caveat. Security is a big issue and most people are afraid to provide any information because of this. Who wants to give strangers so much information about themselves? If banks and other entities are going to be using this technology, then some security systems need to be in place. People and companies are working on this issue, but the wireless LAN security is a work in progress.

BIBLIOGRAPHY

Cairncross, F. (2001). *The Death of Distance: How the Communications Revolution Is Changing Our Lives.* Boston, MA: Harvard Business School Press.

Gast, M. (2002). "Wireless LAN Security: A Short History." Available from <http://www.oreillynet.com/lpt/a/1728>.

Saracco, R., Harrow, J.R., and Weihmayer, R. (2000). *The Disappearance of Tele-communications.* New York: IEEE Press.

Wireless Networks. (2000). Available from <http://portal.acm.org/browse_dl.cfm?linked=1andpart=journalandidx=J804andcoll=portalanddl=ACMandCFID=4757667andCFTOKEN=28643986>.

Y2K

Y2K, millennium bug, doomsday 2000 . . . these and other fearful terms were trumpeted around the world as January 1, 2000, approached. The fear was that a design flaw in computer hardware and software, which only processed dates by saving the last two digits of years, would render the year 2000 indistinguishable from 1900. In the middle to late 1990s, designers woke up to the fact that because countless older systems would still be in use at the dawn of the new millennium, fixing the glitch as newer machines were produced would not solve the problem. Government agencies were especially concerned because many of them were using older equipment.

Thus the Y2K problem took on increasing significance as 2000 approached. In the late 1990s, companies and government agencies spent countless hours and millions of dollars in efforts to correct the problems before the dawn of the millennium. As the actual day approached, tension mounted. Some people declined to make travel plans fearing that airline schedules would be thrown into chaos on January 1. Individuals with medical conditions worried that their caregivers or insurance carriers would be rendered helpless. Rumors of government and commercial catastrophes caused some people to stock up on supplies and food in case commerce ground to a halt.

The event itself was, of course, mercifully anticlimactic. Companies and individuals who prepared for the event suffered no disastrous consequences. Ironically, neither did those who did not prepare. The big event was, for all intents and purposes, a nonevent.

After it was all over, everyone woke up in a world of uninterrupted services. Clearly the dire predictions had come to naught. In the aftermath, a certain amount of anger was directed toward survivalists such as Gary North, who had advised people to move out of urban areas and stockpile supplies in preparation for a millennium melee. Most people, though, simply breathed a sigh of relief, returned to their normal routines, and let the big scare fade from their individual and collective consciousnesses.

BIBLIOGRAPHY

Giles, R. (1999). "Y2K: Balance vs. Sensationalism." *The World and I* 14 (November 1), p. 88.

Whatis.com (2002). "Y2K." *Whatis?com's Encyclopedia of Technology Terms*. Indianapolis, IN: Que.

Index

Page numbers followed by the letter "i" indicate illustrations.

SPECIAL 25%-OFF DISCOUNT!
Order a copy of this book with this form or online at:
http://www.haworthpress.com/store/product.asp?sku=4949

INTERNET AND PERSONAL COMPUTING FADS

_____in hardbound at $29.96 (regularly $39.95) (ISBN: 0-7890-1771-7)

_____in softbound at $11.96 (regularly $15.95) (ISBN: 0-7890-1772-5)

Or order online and use special offer code HEC25 in the shopping cart.

COST OF BOOKS_____

OUTSIDE US/CANADA/
MEXICO: ADD 20%_____

POSTAGE & HANDLING_____
(US: $5.00 for first book & $2.00
for each additional book)
(Outside US: $6.00 for first book
& $2.00 for each additional book)

SUBTOTAL_____

IN CANADA: ADD 7% GST_____

STATE TAX_____
(NY, OH, MN, CA, IN, & SD residents,
add appropriate local sales tax)

FINAL TOTAL_____
(If paying in Canadian funds,
convert using the current
exchange rate, UNESCO
coupons welcome)

☐ **BILL ME LATER:** ($5 service charge will be added)
(Bill-me option is good on US/Canada/Mexico orders only;
not good to jobbers, wholesalers, or subscription agencies.)

☐ Check here if billing address is different from
shipping address and attach purchase order and
billing address information.

Signature_____

☐ **PAYMENT ENCLOSED: $**_____

☐ **PLEASE CHARGE TO MY CREDIT CARD.**

☐ Visa ☐ MasterCard ☐ AmEx ☐ Discover
☐ Diner's Club ☐ Eurocard ☐ JCB

Account # _____

Exp. Date_____

Signature_____

Prices in US dollars and subject to change without notice.

NAME_____

INSTITUTION_____

ADDRESS_____

CITY_____

STATE/ZIP_____

COUNTRY_____ COUNTY (NY residents only)_____

TEL_____ FAX_____

E-MAIL_____

May we use your e-mail address for confirmations and other types of information? ☐ Yes ☐ No
We appreciate receiving your e-mail address and fax number. Haworth would like to e-mail or fax special
discount offers to you, as a preferred customer. **We will never share, rent, or exchange your e-mail address
or fax number.** We regard such actions as an invasion of your privacy.

Order From Your Local Bookstore or Directly From
The Haworth Press, Inc.
10 Alice Street, Binghamton, New York 13904-1580 • USA
TELEPHONE: 1-800-HAWORTH (1-800-429-6784) / Outside US/Canada: (607) 722-5857
FAX: 1-800-895-0582 / Outside US/Canada: (607) 771-0012
E-mailto: orders@haworthpress.com
PLEASE PHOTOCOPY THIS FORM FOR YOUR PERSONAL USE.
http://www.HaworthPress.com

BOF03

DATE DUE